THE LOVE OF MY LIFE

The Memoirs of Howard G. Minsky
with Natalie Garibian Peters

This is the first publication of *The Love of My Life* in any form.

Cover and photo insert design by Curtis Lawyer.

Published by:
The Love of My Life, Inc.
100 Royal Palm Way
Palm Beach, FL 33480

Library of Congress Cataloging-in-Publication Data

ISBN-13 978-0-9789729-0-5

ISBN-10 0-9789729-0-2

LCCN 2006934703

Printed in the United States of America

For Sylvia and My Children

Mervyn LeRoy, famed producer of *The Wizard of Oz*, and my dear friend, would often remind me of the key to making a memorable picture.

"Howard, when you make a movie, in order for it to be successful, that movie has to have heart," he'd say with a twinkle reminiscent of the great Wizard himself. "Just remember it's got to have heart."

CHAPTER 1

In 1936, a very peculiar haze seemed to follow everywhere I went. Perhaps it was the haze of the day, a permanent, lingering reminder of the climate cast by the Depression. Perhaps it was the incessant, impenetrable film of black soot that smothered almost any trace of opportunity in rural Kentucky and the hills of West Virginia, settling itself in the lungs, on the faces and in the deepest dreams of the coal miners with whom I found myself. Was it my own haze of naïve expectation that I had brought winding down with me along the muddy creek roads in my very old and very tired 1933 green Oldsmobile? I was ready to announce my presence, to conquer the back roads and the otherwise forgotten territory that Warner Bros. had assigned me. At twenty-three years old, I was the youngest motion picture salesman on the road, and I was secretly certain, the only one who never before had been away from home.

My job seemed simple enough: sell movies theater to theater; navigate the towns and the characters who inhabited them; tell them about the wondrous Hollywood spectacles that awaited them, all the while, knowing that the very movies I pitched were figments of my own imagination. I had become an expert at concocting storylines, telling elaborate tales to eager theater managers

1

who hung on every descriptive scene, every sound effect I used to punctuate my epics, every mention of a starlet of the day. Motion picture marketing in 1936 was a far cry from the mega-million dollar powerhouse teams pitching movies today. There were no professionally scripted schemes, no flashy one-sheets promising a glimpse of a box office draw with a clever tag line as a call to action. If fact, most of the time there were no movies. I was out there promising films that didn't yet exist.

The studios rarely had projects slated or in production all the time. In order to book a Warner Bros. movie in a theater in the middle of backwoods Kentucky and with no marketing team dictating an approach, the salesman had to rely on his intuition, his cultivated perception of what a particular audience wanted and what the theater owner was willing to buy. The only tool I had was a 15" x 20" book I carried full of studio stills of its stars. The glossies served to prompt me into my stories, and I could gauge based on the theater owner's response to them, which star would make the biggest impression. I'd steal glances around the modest theater and remember who and what I passed driving through town. It was a primitive form of market research, but it worked. As I navigated the roads to my meetings, I'd angle the car's side mirror and watch my face go through a range of emotion as I practiced telling the story of what happens when Bette Davis meets James Cagney in the final scenes of a gritty and dark shoot-em-up, gangster flick. I'd then practice swapping Davis for Kay Francis and rave about the studio's newest release – a heart-pounding thriller aboard the high seas, filled with pirates and rubies and the quintessential damsel in distress. And, as if I, too, was caught in the pirate's wake, I drifted in and out on the theater owners' whims and fancies. If I sensed that they wanted a war-epic, they'd get one — a Howard Minsky action-adventure special, riddled with betrayal and treason, weaponry and romance. To be honest, I could pitch just about anything, and whatever movie with star arrived, the audiences devoured it. I had always used movies as my own personal escape, but until I arrived in my sales territory, Eastern Kentucky as far south at the Tennessee border, I had no idea what escapism really was worth.

I remember the first time I made it up the muddy creek road to the center of a coal mining town. I had my book of stills in the passenger seat while most of the things I owned were shifting in the back as the car struggled over the unpaved drive. My white shirt was still crisp and creased from the wrapping and I was reciting the names of the Warner Bros. contract players in my head. The road gave way to clusters of modest buildings seemingly scattered without thought. They were makeshift dwellings, businesses, homes. I had never seen anything like it. It wasn't uncommon for a home to be a cave with a blanket strung up as a door, and the theaters to which I was to sell my movies were no more than coal camp stores or the local mortuary with large white sheets secured to the wall, the spring hardened chairs on loan from the undertaker. If a proper movie venue existed, it was usually an old mine where an upper balcony and lower orchestra were precariously constructed, an old out-of-tune piano accompanying the cloth screen. I'd learn that balcony admission cost less and was usually reserved for "colored people," but as I saw it, though the balcony symbolized a giant social divide to these people, the escapism afforded by the movies was as big and desired as it was from any vantage point of the seats below.

A miner's low wages allowed for little indulgence. Admission was usually paid in company scrip, a currency that was set up by the mining company and deducted right from their wages. It was a corrupt system. Miners and their families relied on the company for not only setting their pay and handling their accounting, but for virtually all aspects of how their money was spent. The miners used scrip to pay rent for their meager, improvised homes and to purchase necessities like groceries, household goods, tools and clothing in the camp's own general stores. Miners had no control over what they bought or where. Inferior items were sold at inflated prices and this was the norm. Old food would stay on the shelves until the last train that took the coal out of town bothered to show up with replacements.

The men would spend entire days hunched forward, the tops of their heads dusting the low tunnel ceilings as they worked. In the evenings, they'd escape with their families to rickety old chairs, mesmerized by the faces projected against the soft ripple of the old cotton screen. They surrendered to the movies. They lost themselves in an imaginary world in the form of moving images that taunted them with unbounded possibility. Deep, hollow, smoky coughs echoed through the room, but rarely did a miner notice a break in the dialogue, as it was entirely ordinary to ignore all reminders of the very long day in the stale, underground air.

The men loved the war pictures, the police stories and the Westerns, the old Dick Foran singing cowboy movies and the Cagney films revealing a leading man who was unwavering and cool under the pressures of everyday life. Magnified on screen were elegant heroes who stood up to any force that tried to repress them. Soot-stained faces stared, mesmerized by the celluloid; *if only reality mirrored Cagney.* And one thing was a constant, whether in the gilded movie houses of the biggest city or projected onto the dusty bed sheets of the Kentucky mines, both men and women gravitated to a strong leading man, to the complex hero who commanded attention the moment they entered the frame. This stuck out in my mind and would become invaluable for me decades down the road. *The illusive lure of an idol.*

Women loved the heroines – the perfectly coiffed starlets who were flawless on screen, who moved lithely in and out of scenes, captivating the men in their company and never showing any sign that life was hard, or if it was, that it troubled them. How could you not envy that image when your very existence and every possession was obscured, engulfed in the thin, black film of mining life? Movies teased them with clothes that were unlike the make-do rags sold at the commissary. Flawless faces with fancy makeup and lacquered nails weren't palpable where I sold pictures; faint traces of carbon dust would have to do. Men watched actors tout new rifles and

5

fishing lures; the women watched the starlets draped in diamonds and gold, and for a moment, material desires could be satisfied. In that dark room, everyone was transformed into voyeurs, stealing glimpses into never-before-shared secret worlds and convincing themselves deep down that all of those secret desires were attainable. That moment's indulgence on screen would last until the lights flickered on and until I brought the next installment to a place that couldn't be farther away from Hollywood in every way imaginable. I soon realized that I was doing more than selling movies for Warner Bros.; I was the indispensable twenty-five cent gateway to a world of perfection and promise.

Most of my contracts were negotiated with a coal company representative who served as a supervisor for each camp. I'd open my book and point to Edward G. Robinson or Pat O'Brien and tell one story; a few miles down the road, I'd point to the same image and tell one altogether different. Over the years, many movie men have earned reputations of being slick, perhaps curiously superficial. In reality, most couldn't hold a candle to the mining supervisors. There was a terrible sense of undercutting in all of these camps, an underlying feeling of distrust of the company. The miners knew they were being manipulated, but life afforded little chance of standing up to it. There was literally nowhere to run; most of these towns existed exclusively for mining. There was no other industry within its limits. If the residents thought of striking to protest injustices, the coal company would turn off all the electricity in town. I heard a story that once, as a show of just how in control the mining establishment was in the face of the futile protests, the company came in and took all the hinges off the doors of the miners' homes. No one could do a thing about it.

Outside the camps, Union representatives were submitting propaganda to the miners and their families, promoting company agendas and often using scare tactics to motivate allegiance. I remember I had been on the road in Pineville, Kentucky from sun up well into the night and stopped at the local diner for a broiled beef plate. Of course they looked at me funny when I ordered it, and in backwoods culinary fashion, gave me a curly piece of boiled meat still wet in the center of the plate.

I ate it and made my way to my motel room where I was to rehearse my next day's pitches until I fell asleep. I was in my underclothes and making like I was Cagney when a fierce pounding rattled my door.

"Minsky!" the voiced barreled through the pounding. I made my way to the door and opened it a sliver, enough to see the motel manager.

"You got someone in there?" he let his eyes linger over me, stealing a glance into my room which was the size of a large closet and contained everything I owned.

"Jimmy Cagney, Sir."

He squinted his eyes as he did every time I crossed his path. Rightfully so, I suppose; I was the kid from the movies.

"Union's gonna blow this place up tonight. You best get outta here, boy." He made one last look over my shoulder. "You *and* Mr. Cagney."

He stormed to the next door and pounded again.

I latched the door and sat on the bed. I had heard stories about this before. I had been warned to stay clear of their politics. I rested back on the wafer thin pillow. I'd been driving most of the day and the last thing I wanted to do was to spend the night in the Olds. I had a meeting first thing in the morning and, well, *how likely was it, really, that I'd be blown to smithereens there in Pineville, Kentucky?*

I went to the window, drew back the shades and watched motel guests scurry across the dead lawn to their cars, children and belongings scattered. The manager's fist echoed as he made his last few obligatory appeals, and slowly the people and the pounding trailed off; silence fell over the abandoned property. As I had done on so many nights in obscure motel rooms, I said a prayer and fell asleep hoping that the next morning I'd be back on the road.

I didn't blow up in the motel. In fact, the attempt was a typical tactic devised to shake up the stability of the township — backwoods terrorism that usually worked. Perhaps I was too naïve to understand the implications; perhaps I was childishly defiant in wanting to keep my plans the next day. The next morning I headed to my car with the picture book tucked under my arm, deciding if my first pitch was going to be a dusty, suspenseful Western or a cop caper with the most spectacular shootout Pineville had ever seen. That was the first time my life would be threatened.

I've thought a lot about that night over the past seventy years. This was the climate in which I worked selling escapism. This was why I couldn't possibly make up a story that wouldn't sell.

I covered at least fifty thousand miles a year meandering through unpaved creek beds, sometimes bypassing entire towns and appointments when the roads were just too wet to navigate. The cost of four secondhand tires ran a respectable fifteen dollars in 1936, and I had become not only an expert in negotiating for them, but changing them myself. I kept extra, white-collared shirts in the back seat for this reason. I learned quickly how to be out on the road alone. Most of my colleagues were in their forties and fifties, and though they often singled me out for being young and ambitious, I never let them confuse my hunger with immaturity. There was a degree of resentment in many of my relationships on the road, for I was a kid after all, a kid who got his start through his successful show business uncle. I became programmed to pick up on underlying resentment, and became more adept at overachieving to prove that I had earned my place once the preverbal door had been opened for me. After all, I *needed* to be understood. I was alone in Kentucky with these men, and whether I liked it or not, they would become my extended family. I would eat and live and commute with them. We'd attend studio conventions and trade stories of near misses and near triumphs. They'd call me "The Kid," and I didn't mind being "The Kid" as long as they knew I was no different from them while out on the road.

I loved being out there. My other option was staying in Philadelphia, working local odd jobs to earn a living. I knew what was happening at home. My father was out of work and most fathers in the neighborhood faced the same thing. It was a tough time; jobs weren't easy to come by, and here I was being paid to wander through the South, to make up fabulous stories, to wear a movie studio badge that implied that I was somehow part of something big. I didn't mind that I had to send my paycheck home; I was in show business and I was "The Kid."

I remember finding myself alone with my father during a visit home. He asked me what it was like to be on the road, to be the youngest one out there.

"They know I work hard, dad," I told him.

"Good."

"But they always call me 'pretty boy'," I finished, lifting my brow to see him lower his.

"Why do you say that about yourself?" he started.

"*I* don't say it, they do."

"Well put it out of your mind."

Dad was a man's man. His son was no "pretty boy," though over the years, my changing appearance garnered attention, mostly unwanted and usually embarrassing. I had always secretly admired the screen idols I had grown up with, well-dressed, hair slicked in place, a cool and confident gait. Whether these influences crept into my maturing I don't know, but I was always teased about my appearance. And my father, I suppose, wanted to remind me that I was a film salesman, not a movie star.

"Pretty Boy" and "The Kid" were things I could handle, but I wasn't yet ready to understand the depths of human behavior or the ignorance that often comes along with it.

It was one of the smaller towns and I was sitting with an old miner who was now the camp boss. He was flipping through my book grunting and commenting under his breath at the glossy images captured undoubtedly on a studio lot somewhere in Southern California. I had met men like this before, unimpressed with anything to which he did not belong nor subscribe. But more powerful than that mindset was the businessman in him who knew he could get fifteen to twenty-five cents per miner for every screening; and, as a businessman myself, I wasn't about to let him forget that.

I mentioned to him the incredible popularity of the last few Edward G. Robinson pictures and even threw in a comment or two about the town over and just how packed their theaters had become from the latest Warner Bros. release. He looked me up and down, his furrowed brow contorting his already leathered face.

"Your name Minsky?" he grunted again.

"Yes," I answered.

"What's that, Russian?" The miner crossed his bony arms and waited. Surely, he had sized me up correctly.

"I'm Jewish."

The miner didn't move, save a twitch in one eye. He watched me. I felt him studying every dark hair on my head, every pore of my tanned skin. As if I had just appeared in front of him that moment, he leaned back, arms still crossed.

"You a Jew? Well I'll be goddamned. I never seen a Jew before. You really a Jew?" He waited for my response. I thought for sure he would prod me to confirm that I was, in fact, flesh and bones.

"I really am," I said slowly. I couldn't be sure what would come next. I was undoubtedly one of the only Jews, if not the only one, in the entire territory at that moment. The last time I was confronted about being a Jew was when I was eight years old in the basement of the Lutheran Church down our street. I was playing basketball and a kid called me Jew in a tone I had never heard before. I didn't know why, but I socked him. I kept hitting him harder and harder until my brother pulled me off of him.

The miner examined me.

"Well I'll be damned. Guess we got all kinds of people comin' round here." He thought a moment and looked down at the book; Kay Francis stared back with two of the most beautiful eyes in pictures. The miner sighed, "I guess I'll sign the contract anyhow."

I ran over the words in my head on the way home, once or twice tilting the rearview mirror down to look myself over. I was always conscious that people looked at me funny when I walked into town. Perhaps it was the requisite sales uniform: creased shirt, dark slacks and tie. Maybe it was what I represented — an industry seemingly full of perfect people and lives. Or maybe it was just me: a city kid who just didn't understand the world in which he was now living.

I'd dismiss much of it to the fact that I was a stranger in a stranger land. I was quick and well-spoken, confident in the properties I represented, and ultimately, an urban salesman who had nothing to do with, nor no way to understand, the untouched way of life in the mining camps. In one area called Brethet County I was given a very stern warning not to stay in town after sundown. My imagination ran wild with scenarios of Union representatives making an example of me or my wandering the wrong way into a mine and trapping myself at the bottom of a dark and abandoned shaft. The realties were far less romantic. The warning was disguised as a measure to keep the young salesman safe in an unfamiliar place. The truth was that it was one of their own tactics to keep the town safe from the unfamiliar stranger. What better way to corrupt or sideline the efforts of mining life than by bringing in a book of pictures promising that things outside the town were beautiful and attainable.

"Stay away from our women," lingered over my shoulder.

I was a member of the Variety Club which was one of the affiliations I've most enjoyed in my life. The Variety Club started in Pittsburgh in 1927 and has a very interesting beginning. Originally it was named by the eleven men who started it as a social club. They rented a room at the William Penn Hotel, which would have a deep significance to me not too far down the road. A curious, and some say miraculous, thing happened on Christmas Eve 1928 which not only drew international attention, but which is probably the underlying reason the organization still exists today. That night, a one month old baby was abandoned in one of the seats of the Sheridan Square Theater, owned by one of the Variety Club founding members. A note was attached to the

13

baby's clothing saying her name was Catherine and that she was born on Thanksgiving Day. Her mother had eight other children and her husband was out of work. Counting on the "goodness of show business people," she abandoned her daughter. The note was signed *"A Heartbroken Mother."*

When her parents couldn't be located, the club members decided to become responsible for her upbringing. Baby Catherine became Catherine Variety Sheridan, after the group which took her in and the theater in which she was found. Needless to say, baby Catherine received attention and donations from all over the world — so many that the founders decided to make Catherine's overwhelming support available for other underprivileged children. The good feeling Catherine brought was infectious and immediately others in show business wanted to be involved.

I had a chance to join this group when I was in my early twenties and I fondly remember being so proud to be part of a business that had pooled its tremendous resources and influence to help those who couldn't help themselves.

The only tainted memory I have of the Variety Club was that of Otto Brown, a theater owner from Kentucky with whom I had regularly conducted business. Otto was a sharp man and was as hardened as the others who lived and worked amongst the mines. We were in Cincinnati for a Variety convention and I recall walking into the Netherland Hotel and immediately seeing a lovely girl who was garnering a great deal of attention from everyone in the room. Before I could extend my hand to greet Otto, he pulled me by the sleeve and with a finger in my chest made it very clear that I was to stay away from his daughter or that he would kill me.

For quite some time I mistook these warnings as a misinterpretation of my actions or my intentions. After all, I hadn't stopped hearing the warnings over my shoulder to not get involved or too interested in mining life or the women that anchored it. It wasn't until I had dinner in the home of West Virginia theater owner Garland West, a rare invitation to an outsider, that I learned otherwise. They didn't fear what I, myself, would do. Rather, more simply, I was a constant reminder of another world that existed for anyone who could make it far enough down the road.

I felt like an important guest in the home of Garland West. His wife prepared a dinner of fried eggs and each member of the family watched me eat. When the meal was over I rose from the table and began clearing the dishes. The room fell silent and Garland put his leathered hand on mine, pointing at his wife and daughters as if to say they were there for that purpose. I smiled respectfully and made my way into the kitchen to help them wash the dishes. He watched me suspiciously through the opening to the kitchen as I brandished a dish towel and made pleasant conversation with the hostess.

It was these differences of lifestyle that took me some time to understand. The fear and distrust of young Howard Minsky was not an assessment of my character or my intentions, rather the precautionary defense against letting in even a trickle of an unknown world. I was the bearer of these worldly things, and perhaps, if they never shook my hand, they'd never have to know that my world really existed. It was an innate paranoia to protect their wives, children and, secretly, even themselves, from the seduction of the independence and abandon they knew existed from my movies, but that they couldn't afford to let infiltrate their only known way of life.

Garland West asked me to stay the night and I slept in a small spare room that I knew was a luxury. The windows were missing the glass and I could hear lingering on the humid breeze, the voice of someone singing an old mining tune. It was a grown man's gravel voice, tainted by the burden of time. It was a song about a child, standing at his doorway, watching his father head off to the mine. The child cried after his father, shouting for him to come back. *Come back,* because everyone knows that fathers forget about their children and their wives and are never seen again, swallowed up by the dark, deep belly of the mine. The song was hymnal, telling.

I curled up on the tattered, hard mattress and thought about life if it meant waking up here every day. The haunting song lulled me to sleep. *Come back, daddy... promise you'll come back, promise you'll remember me after today.*

CHAPTER 2

Things picked up for my family while I was on the road. I'd call back every week to relay my stories, intentionally censoring anything that would cause my mother to worry more than usual. It was in 1937 that my Uncle Harry got my father a position as a theater manager in Philadelphia. Though we still sent home most of our pay, this new source of income allowed my brothers and me to use some of our money any way we wished. My little sister Evelyn was a bright spot on the days I called home, her high-pitched voice on the other end of the phone always insisting I tell her about the fabulous movies I was brokering and all the beautiful heroines I had come to know so well. I'd always save a story for Evelyn, sometimes based in truth, oftentimes a Howard elaboration, but always something that she clung to and repeated to everyone in Philadelphia as fact from her big brother in show business. It was innocuous gossip, like how the starlets coiffed their hair or how good sleep and a glass of milk made her favorite actress radiant. I told her that I always wanted her to take care of herself and I promised to send her two dollars a week to have her nails manicured. Evelyn thought that was the most spectacular indulgence of which she had ever heard, and I reminded her that nice girls don't bite their nails; I didn't want my sister branded a nail-biter. As I promised, my newly expendable income went to Evelyn, and I heard through my mother that she'd lie in bed with her arms outstretched, staring up at her shiny fingernails with a perpetual grin on her sweet, young face.

What I had left of my modest pay helped keep me afloat out on the road. One afternoon I was driving on a Kentucky highway when a coal truck blindsided me and smashed into my driver's side. It happened so fast. I managed to squeeze myself from the crushed door and made my way to the side of the road where the old coal truck had pulled over. The driver had his head in his hands and I waved mine wildly, spouting and spewing more steam that my Olds, kicking its tires and watching the miner slowly and cautiously approach me. The more I flailed my arms at him, the more I accepted that I had dislocated my shoulder. I began waving only one arm.

"What in the world were you thinking?" I screamed. The miner lowered his head and looked at my car. Half of it was crushed.

"You alright sir?"

What?

"I'm sorry, sir." He looked me in the eye. I looked back at his truck. The front was flattened.

A State Trooper pulled up and looked us both over before getting out of the patrol car. He made a few notes on his pad and stepped out. He lingered over both vehicles and approached the miner. I leaned against the remaining solid side of the Oldsmobile and rubbed my right shoulder.

What in the world was he investigating? The situation couldn't have been more obvious.

"Mornin', young man," the officer tilted his head back to see my flushed face from under his brimmed hat.

"Not really," I sputtered back.

"Reasonable tone, I do understand, but I've been lookin' into this here accident and nothin' we decide to do right here is going to help you."

Did I mention that things are brutally matter-of-fact in the South? I stood incredulous.

"He's got no 'nsurance, Mr. Minsky. The man's been drivin' this third-hand truck longer'n you've been alive. It's all he's got and between you and me, it ain't worth taking from him."

The driver was now in the passenger seat of his grimy truck, his head slumped forward on the dashboard. The officer stole his own glance in my backseat.

"You livin' in there, boy?" he craned his neck for a better look.

"Pretty much," I answered.

"No sense in both of you being homeless now, is there?" The officer locked his eyes with mine. I had already come to the conclusion that I had no use for a third-hand coal truck or for putting an old man out of business.

"No, sir. No sense." I said it reluctantly and then accepted the trooper's offer to take me to the hospital to reset my shoulder.

Despite my immediate frustrations, financially and of inconvenience, there was something very satisfying in the relief on the driver's face when the officer waved him clearance to go. It is a very hard life with grueling days mining and transporting coal; this setback would have undoubtedly derailed him for good. I wondered a lot about him over the years, about how many trips up and down the muddy roads he'd need to make to pay for that accident. I also wondered if he sometimes secretly wished that I had taken his very lifeblood away from him for good.

CHAPTER 3

Whether people were lined up to sit on red velvet seats or undertakers' chairs on loan, whether they looked up at enormous images in dazzling movie houses or grew used to the subtle ripple of the bed sheet screen, one thing remained true – movies belonged to everyone, as much to the miner and his family as they did to the city socialite internalizing her own escapism in that dark and anonymous theater.

I understood completely what took over when the lights were dimmed and the flicker of film begins to hypnotize. I make it sound like we are helpless, being lulled unknowingly into another world, but in truth, we are willing participants. By virtue of being there and allowing movies and their industry to take over our consciousness, we surrender our realities to whatever might come in the dark. It happened to me, over and over as a child, and I decided one day that I would surrender completely to the business that had opened a new world for me and for many I knew during a time when realities of life, politics and human behavior were sometimes not so perfect.

I was born on Robinson Street in West Philadelphia in 1914 as war broke out in Europe. My father came from Russia when he was four and my mother around the same age from Lithuania. My mother, Sarah, made the trip across the sea in steerage class, a far cry from the Bette Davis epics I had painted aboard exquisite ships with moonlight drenching wood-stained decks. Rather, her journey came with little more than Russian black bread that my grandmother soaked in vinegar, meant to be a sedative, to smell and taste during the rocky nights in the middle of the ocean alone.

My father, Jacob, or Jack as he was called, was a quiet and mindful man who, like me, started supporting his family on the road. He sold candy and refreshments on the Reading Railroad trains, up and down the aisles like his son would mirror in Philadelphia's dark theaters years later. Dad would tell us about the winding journey he made up and back on the rails with the world changing through one window, and on the return, predictably becoming familiar again. His limitations of language were inconsequential most of the time, as he limited elaborate interaction with the passengers and studied the names on the food wrappers to make sure he could identify the items asked for. A large tray dangled from his thin neck by a sweat-stained strap. To some, the burden of selling concessions on a train to nowhere would be mindless work, but as I later learned with five nickels and a flashlight, the train to nowhere afforded my father a journey into another world. The most elegant, gloved women accompanied businessmen who read newspapers while everything familiar passed outside the windows. Dad was right there to see that there were as many kinds of passengers as there were stops along the way. Nameless characters entered and exited his days as they did mine. I would ultimately be given a piece of the great American dream that dad had humbly secured for me on the Reading Rail.

Dad was promoted to the manager of the Union News Company that stood at the foot of Market Street in Philadelphia. At the Delaware River, before the bridge was ever built, he sold newspapers, cigarettes and sundries to passersby, again internalizing the hurried anonymity of city life. My mother stressed heavily the need to be educated in a world that was up for grabs. She was very dedicated to the American way and read as much as she could as her self-taught English developed. We'd usually know exactly what mom read because she was a very good source of news and gossip. To earn money as a girl, she worked in a tobacco factory rolling cigars, a job that was available to young Eastern European immigrants at the time. I've had secret moments throughout my life when I lingered on the taste of the infrequent cigar, most of the time to mark a milestone in my professional life. I never once lost sight of where that cigar came from and what the person who rolled it could have possibly wanted out of life. As a child, I respected my parents because that's the type of home in which we were raised. As a man, I respected my parents because I learned, being out there alone, that it was hard enough to make a name for yourself when you were born American and spoke English. For my parents, and for so many others that started the industries we now run, life in America began much like the silent pictures I loved as a kid – a communication barrier holding back an undoubtedly fantastic storyline. I have the utmost respect for those determined enough to conquer those fundamental setbacks, destined to emerge as a defining part of the culture and community.

I was the middle child of two brothers. Joe was the oldest and perfect in every way, and Teddy, my kid brother, had the best temperament and heart of any man I have ever known. The baby was our sister Evelyn, the Minsky Princess, and once I thought I had killed her.

I remember being given my first role of responsibility when Evelyn was three and I swore up and down to my mother that I could handle taking her to the park by myself. Forty-five minutes later I carried her into the house, blood from her face covering her little, yellow dress. She wouldn't stop screaming and I was so shaken up, I passed her to my mother like she was the hot potato. I was pushing her on the swings, everything was going so well and I was the biggest brother alone at the park. And then, while at the crest of an upswing, she fell forward and onto the playground dirt. She lay still for a moment and I didn't know what to do. I thought for sure that I had done something terrible. I tried to make up for it once when the Hamilton School bully dangled a mangled, dead mouse in Teddy's face and called the other kids around to watch him cry. Teddy clenched his eyes and wept, unable to move as the kid threatened to throw the rat on him if he budged. He just dangled it there, moving it closer and closer until its whiskers touched Teddy's button nose. I stepped in and threatened to sock the bully. All he did was put the rat to my face and I realized that he could wipe the floor with me. Teddy and I were now both screaming and our big brother Joe had to squash him for the both of us. That wasn't he first time Joe stepped in. When we moved from South Philadelphia to West Philadelphia I became friends with a boy named Al, who we called "The Greek" and who was considerably bigger than I. No one ever knew whether he was Greek or not, but somewhere along the road, he became the only eleven-year-old with a moniker. We were playing marbles and he claimed he hit my shooter and won it. Fire raged in me and before I knew it I had initiated the first fight in my life. I lost my head and went wild on "The Greek" and, though not a recommended resolution noted in the Queensberry rules, I was vindicated, considered myself the winner and left him the shooter to remember me by. It was a lesson in sticking together and a lesson in picking your fights wisely that I would heavily rely upon in the future.

Aside from the bloody noses and the bloody dresses, my family was a fantastic, built-in audience for my antics and early business ventures. I learned early on the value of being resourceful in a family with four children. Everyone had his or her own interests and hobbies, allowing me to disappear from the center of attention and go into business for myself. I was maybe eight or nine years old when I started collecting my mother's belongings I considered to be junk. When she was busy with my siblings, I'd slip from view and rummage through her closets, keepsakes and kitchen. I'd arrange a stockpile in my bedroom and cover it with an old blanket. When the time was right, I'd take her "junk" and go door-to-door in the neighborhood selling her things and opting for straight pins over money. Straight pins were the fabulous silver-colored currency I determined I'd collect, and as I stood in someone's doorway with my mother's colander, I'd negotiate just how many of the woman's sewing pins I could get for something I found totally useless. I'd take my junk to the front yard and in an inconspicuous place, I'd describe to my friends in my elementary sales pitch why I thought they needed my clothing and old toys and why they needed to get their mothers' straight pins to purchase such a valuable find. I'd sit on my bedroom floor and count and recount all the glittering pins that I had accumulated. If I had known what the word entrepreneur meant, I'd have used one of those fabulous pins to fasten the label to my shirt.

That wouldn't be the first endeavor to land me in serious trouble at home. I broke my leg when I was six years old and was confined to a ridiculous plaster cast. Rendered virtually immobile, I'd sit in one place in the living room and stare out the window at others moving freely outside. One of those afternoons, my eye caught on our living room furniture and I became fixated with just how unattractive the solid wooden legs were to me. I hopped on one leg to the dining table and ran my hands over the leg of thick, dark wood, studying the grain, the joints, the unnecessary heaviness. Surely, I thought that the straight angle of the wood could be improved upon. It took all afternoon, hopping from the dining room to the family room, back and forth, surveying my work, positioning my cast. I had sculpted, whittling with a large kitchen knife, a new, modern, rounded-leg set of dining table, chairs and sofa. The floor was covered in wood shavings when my mother came in to find me balancing on my good leg, knife in hand, shaving the last heavy detail from my furniture masterpiece. All the pieces were now precariously perched on awkward, uneven, jagged branches.

When I got a little older my mother decided that I ought to play outside more and I began to socialize with the other kids in the neighborhood. I instantly found a captive audience in the local children, the youngest ones wide-eyed and curious as I told them about fantastic stories I had heard, never letting them know that I had made them up in my own head. That lead to a brief stint as the Robinson Street producer who put on his own plays, cast his friends and charged straight pins for admission. I watched my visions materialize on the sidewalks, but my neighborhood theater business was shut down while I was still a significant draw. It was time, my father had decided, that I take a real job. When other kids were being sent off to summer camp, I went to work.

My first position was at the local A & P where I had the illustrious responsibility of packaging one pound buckets of lard. One has no idea how long the greasy feeling of lard lingers between your fingers until you spend every day scooping it and smoothing it into containers. Luck would have it that my big brother Joe had a job at a fruit and vegetable market in our town. He got me a position that I had no idea ever existed. I was to dress the displays, but more than stack potatoes and melons, I was in charge of the cosmetics. I was to trim the brown edges from the lettuce, to freshen up their appearance. Sometimes you could tell which lettuce was mine by the jagged edges I managed to tuck under other obscure leaves. I shined the apples with a white cotton cloth until they glimmered like red lights piled atop one another. I had no idea that this job would prepare me for anything else in my life, but fate would dictate down the road that I was to dress up yet-to-be-made movies with the same subtle manipulation that my apples and lettuce required.

In addition to the fruit stand, I would work for two dollars a Saturday in the local department store hanging up ladies' coats. Most of them were twice my size and a few of them were exceptionally smelly. I'd learn the proper way to hang them, to lace the scarf through the arm, and, my least favorite part, how to put them back on their owners. I learned the difference between certain fabrics (most notably which were the heaviest and which breathed least) and became adept at spotting a coat on the street and knowing whose name was on the label. If I worked overtime, I'd get fifty cents for dinner. In the winter I'd shovel snow with my brothers or headed out with my Flexible Flyer sled that my parents budgeted to buy me for my birthday. In the summer, when I wasn't working, I'd join in neighborhood stickball even though I wasn't that good at it.

Then came an opportunity that would undoubtedly change my life forever. The Spruce

Street Theater wasn't too far from home and even if I had no business near it, I made a point to detour past on most days. I was enthralled not only by the few movies I had seen in my short life, but by the talk I had heard about all the ones I was never able to see. One afternoon, I let myself wander from the sidewalk into the theater and sat in the cold and dark room, looking up at nothing. We couldn't afford to take the whole family to the movies often, but the images I had seen lingered in my memory to that very moment. In the hollow, empty room I heard the echoing of wooden soles coming closer.

"You like movies, kid?" a tall, thin man whispered from the row behind me. I turned to see him studying me. I shrugged.

"You want to see 'em for free?" he offered.

"Nothing's free, sir." I spit back the mantra I had learned the hard way in my string of jobs and at home carving furniture. He came around and took the seat next to me. He pointed at me square in the chest and smiled.

"You're smart, kid. And you're right. But how 'bout I give you a very important job that would let you earn a seat for any movie I have in this theater?"

I was floored. Did such a job really exist?

"You circulate my programs all over the neighborhood and I let you watch as many movies as your eyes and your mother will let you." I sat there waiting to hear the drawback, but nothing more came. I sized him up – dark slacks, white shirt and a tie. A tie meant to my seven year old mind that he had the very right to make this offer.

"Are you in charge here?" I asked, an

29

unusually developed skepticism in my very young voice.

"Yes, I am," he said.

I had never heard something so wonderful in my life.

It was hard enough sitting through school on a normal day, but on my first day employed by the theater, I couldn't think of anything but that afternoon when I would get my hands on those flyers. I'd set off to tell the whole neighborhood, not only what films were coming to town, but rather, that Howard Minsky was officially in show business. I'd spend every day after school going house-to-house slipping the theater's circulars under neighbors' doors. The programs announced the coming attractions and would often highlight a particular star or current feature. To be completely honest, I didn't much care what they said as long as the manager kept his end of the deal and I could spend every extra hour I had on Spruce Street. I went door-to-door until I had to be home for dinner, and sometimes, when it got too cold, or it got too late, I'd unload handfuls of programs into the sewer or use them to make an armament of paper airplanes.

I remember the first time I saw a movie, having earned, myself, the right to be there. It was empowering to enter the movie house and walk past the ticket girl who knew I was someone official. While others lined up and paid for tickets, I excused myself past them, looking back once or twice to see if they were looking at me, wondering who that boy was who belonged there. I slipped into the back of the theater and immediately my life changed. In all my eight-year-old glory I glued my eyes to the grainy images on the screen as they ticked by with the hum of the projector and the piano music. The most spectacular world was within my grasp and I decided that afternoon that I would never let go of it.

I couldn't wait for Saturdays and for the release of the new Western serials. I'd be reacquainted with my favorite cowboy stars like Tom Mix and Art Accord, names that had become permanent figures in my private world. I'd sit low in the springy seat and hum along with every Western whistle, wide-eyed with every pseudo pistol POP the music affected. I couldn't believe my good fortune. It seemed like it was just yesterday that I was wrist deep in A&P lard buckets and now I was an accepted and welcomed member of the movies. There was nothing like sitting by myself, watching Gary Cooper, with half my stack of programs shoved down the front of my pants. Apparently no one ever caught on, because I was promoted from flyer distributor to a position as an usher in a much larger Warner Bros. chain theater. I was in Junior High School and it was the greatest job a kid could ask for. Not only was I constantly in the company of the greatest faces on screen, but I got to wear a military-like uniform and I had the awesome responsibility of carrying five nickels in case anyone had to make a phone call. I felt like top sergeant. I was making $12.82 a week.

I was thirteen years old when my mother called me into the living room and said that I'd received a surprise from Uncle Harry. She held out two tickets to the Fox-Locust Theater in

Philadelphia. I couldn't believe it; I was going to see my first talking movie!

I couldn't remember the last time I'd seen mom dress up, but that night she looked so pretty. I could tell that even though she wasn't bouncing in her plush red chair like I was, she was excited to be there. The theater was ornately gilded and a far cry from the local movie houses where I had fallen in love with film.

The lights dimmed and I could barely contain myself – images were flickering in sync with sound that didn't come from an old out-of-tune piano, rather it seemed, right from the mouths of the actors. I watched *The Jazz Singer* that night and never took my eyes off the screen until the last frame flicked by. The audience was equally mesmerized. When Al Jolson sang "Mamie" and his mouth moved in song, you could hear the patrons gasp, even whisper disbelief. When it was over, the audience stood and cheered, and there in the Fox-Locust Theater in 1927, I knew I would never be the same.

After a while, talking pictures arrived at my theater. Though I had been bragging about *The Jazz Singer* to just about everyone who would listen, no one would understand what a talking movie was until they saw it for themselves. The response was unbelievable. As an usher I'd have to quiet the audience, as undoubtedly, every time a new movie screened, patrons discussed the new entertainment "miracle." We five ushers, dressed like Boy Scouts, would march up and down the aisles with the beams of our flashlights creeping over the faces fixed up at the screen. I'd escort patrons to their seats, up and down, day and night, the whole time replaying the same dialogue in my head until I knew every line by heart. My lips would move in sync with the actors' words, and in some way, I was an eager puppet on the most intriguing stage I could imagine. Line by line, I took movies as my own. Word by word, I internalized them and unknowingly became a filmmaker.

Ushering became more colorful with the advent of sound in movies. There were frequent moments when the audio would fall out of synch with the picture and the audience would shout and sometimes throw whatever they had on hand. Our responsibility was to maintain order while the technician scrambled to cue the record that held the film's sound separate from the celluloid. Amidst all the commotion, I secretly laughed at how marvelous it all really was.

While in high school I took the position of assistant manager of the Columbia Theater in town. I couldn't believe I was making $17.00 a week doing something I was made for. Now a manager, others looked at me differently, as if I knew something more than I did as an usher, and sometimes I secretly wondered if I should. I was still the same kid, but instead of keeping quiet with my flashlight in the dark, I was greeting patrons and overseeing other kids, some who loved the movies as much as I. Since I devoured every new release and would sometimes sit alone after my shift and watch them over again, I was able to pass along my opinions of the movies and even tease some of the patrons with a taste of the dialogue I had learned by heart.

"And John Gilbert was just mad about

Garbo. The hottest star of silent films and then when talkies took of and the studio found out that Gilbert had a voice like a little girl, well, that was the end of Gilbert and certainly the end of his love affair with Garbo," I told my family over dinner as if I was told by Greta Garbo herself. My father looked back down at his plate. Movies were infiltrating not only our home but the Depression Era as a whole. In a time when luxuries and lightheartedness were scarce, movies became more popular than ever, offering escapism and possibilities secretly wished for in every dark theater.

The scarcity of money also conditioned my choice to not go to college. The only interest I had outside of movies was a curiosity of medicine sparked by a good friend of mine who was at Jefferson Medical School. I wasn't a scholar by any stretch, in fact, I nearly didn't graduate from high school because I couldn't grasp physics as taught to me by an old man who had as much personality as my buckets of lard. He had to give me a special exam at the end of the year that would decide if I graduated or not, and I made it by the skin of my teeth. I kept physics and the requisite premed courses in mind as my friend brought me to the Medical School for a tour and as a guest to watch several live surgeries. The operations were fascinating, though I thought at first I wouldn't be able to handle them. I knew that going to college was an impossibility. My paycheck and those of my brothers' were helping the family stay afloat.

"I drove a cab all four years, Howard. You can do that, too, and make plenty of money for school," my friend offered. For a split second, while watching a throat surgery, I considered it, but I knew it wasn't right. My family needed me and I needed the movies.

I loved being a manager, but one day I got a call from my Uncle Harry who was an executive on the theater circuit in New York. My parents told him of my infatuation with movies, and he asked if I was interested in really learning about show business. I told him that I was earning a whole $17.00 a week. He arranged a meeting for me at Warner Bros. for a sales position covering territory from Eastern Kentucky to the southern Tennessee border.

"Lonely meals and lonelier motel rooms," he told me, but if I stuck with it and loved it, I'd see a lot more than $17.00 a week in show business.

CHAPTER 4

In the early part of 1937 I got a call from my older brother Joe who was working in Pittsburgh as a salesman for the Moleta paint company. He was effortlessly handsome, a popular athlete in school and very good with people. We spoke regularly on the phone but Joe was never one to ask me for dating advice or anything remotely close to it. He insisted that I come to Pittsburgh as soon as possible to meet a girl that he had seen a few times.

"What do you want me to meet her for if you're dating her?" I asked from a motel phone somewhere near the Tennessee border. Girls had always flocked to Joe and my opinion of them never seemed to matter.

"I just want you to meet her," he said cryptically.

I don't know why I went, but I found myself the next week on a blind, double date with Joe, the girl he was seeing, and a friend of hers. I was never really into this sort of thing, in fact, I'd spent more time in the company of Bette Davis and coal miners than I had double-dating on the town. The life of a salesman is a rather simple one but becomes very complex if you have to explain it to someone else. It would take a special girl to understand why I lived out of the car most of the year.

I was raised to be a gentleman, but something in me kept me from paying mind to my date, a lovely girl named Caddy Lieberman. There was nothing wrong with her. In fact, had the circumstances been within my control, she would have made a lovely dinner companion. Rather, the moment I met my brother's girlfriend, Sylvia, I knew that I would only be fixated on one thing that night. I noticed out of the corner of my eye that Caddy was watching me over her untouched dinner, sizing up this seemingly arrogant stranger who whisked into town to ignore her. I was watching Joe interact with his date, following every refined motion she made, tracing her porcelain face with my eyes. She was petite, brunette and had crystal blue eyes that crinkled at the corners when she smiled. Joe was, without a doubt, the luckiest guy in the world.

I exchanged pleasantries with Caddy as she watched other couples make way to the dance floor. The music was perfect and I had traveled all this way; it was now or never.

"Would you like to dance?" I blurted out across the table to Sylvia. Mid-sentence Joe turned to me and I could see he was suppressing a faint smile. Sylvia looked from Joe to me, hesitated a moment, then stood. In a seamless second, Joe took up conversation with Caddy, who hid her displeasure of me in her cocktail.

I escorted Sylvia to the dance floor, the beat of the music replacing my missing heartbeat. She let me lead and I could feel her hands were cold and small; when she wasn't looking I stole a glance at her shiny fingernails. Caddy's head bobbed and tilted and her hands punctuated what was undoubtedly a colorful exchange, but Joe seemed to humor her as he, too, watched Sylvia and me across the room. I tried to suppress it, but my imagination took over. If only this picture were in my book of stills, I'd have no trouble finishing off the epic I had been dreaming up while watching Sylvia all night laughing next to Joe.

"You're not a bad dancer," her voice cut across the music. My confidence swelled and I immediately started improvising steps I'd never seen before. She giggled, even laughed at me, but I kept moving, kept imagining myself in top hat and tails on the arm of the most beautiful girl in the room. I spun her and dipped her and her milky face became flushed, her breathing a little hurried. At some point that evening, after hours of her undivided attention, I started to hope that it had nothing to do with my dancing. *Could she possibly find me interesting?* Joe had told her that I lived on the road, that I spent my days in obscure theaters and my nights in and out of more obscure diners and motels. She was intrigued, curious as to what I was looking for out on the road by myself. I had never thought about it that way. I didn't think I was looking for anything. What does a twenty-three year old kid know to look for if he doesn't know it exists to begin with? Sylvia leaned in to me at the table, rendering Joe and Caddy out of earshot.

"You have a lovely brother," she whispered. *What did that mean?*

"He is lovely." It's all I could think to say. *I knew I was dancing like a fool.*

"But you're lovely, too, Howard." And,

as quickly as it was ruined, my life was perfect again.

"Are you serious with her?", I asked Joe when the ladies excused themselves together.

"Come on, Howie, I'm not serious with anyone," he said and raised his glass to me. "I just wanted you to meet her, that's all. She's a really nice girl. A really good girl, Howie."

I knew he was right, but I also knew that a girl like Sylvia wouldn't keep Joe single for very long. She and Caddy meandered their way back through the tables and I tried to act like I hadn't seen them. The one time I allowed myself to look up at her, I found Sylvia's eyes locked on mine.

Sometimes I sit in alone in my den and think about that night and how very simple love was at that moment. Was it because we didn't know any better? Was it because at the core of something pure and right, it's designed to be easy? I knew in me that Joe had called me to Pittsburgh that night because I was supposed to be there. I apologized repeatedly to Caddy Lieberman and, I think, deep down, she understood what happened over those few short hours.

Sylvia allowed me the honor of flying into Pittsburgh three more times in the next two months to see her. I was the best salesman I had ever been in those weeks, but once or twice the guys wondered why I kept pitching love epics and not my best Minsky shoot-em-up Western. I suppose I turned to mush in some way, but I didn't care. Secretly, I kind of liked it, knowing that at the end of the day, after I piled my book of faces into the car and finished off my reports, I had someone to call to say goodnight.

On my third trip back to see Sylvia, I found myself loitering the manicured sidewalk outside her parents' home for what seemed like half an hour. I stared up at the three-story home with the weathered porch swing creaking in the breeze, cast in a glow from a light in the highest window. I knew somehow that that window was Sylvia's, and at that very moment, I almost turned and walked away. I had rehearsed in my mind all the things I would say when I walked into that house, convincing myself that it was no more difficult than all the other stories I had ever told. Before I could commit to one, the porch light flicked on and the door opened.

"Howard, is that you?" her mother leaned over the threshold and craned her neck to see me standing in the middle of the sidewalk, mid-pace.

"Yes, Mrs. Shear, uh, good evening."

"Howard, what are you doing in the street?" her voice carried into the night and I looked up to the window to see an angel's face watching me in the dark road.

She let me in and excused herself into the kitchen. I heard whispers trail from behind the closed kitchen door. It made me more nervous to think that they were all waiting for me to do something stupid and, of course, debating as to why I was out in the street. I busied myself in the only thing I could find near me, the heavy velvet drapes, and as if I had cultivated a longtime obsession with stitching, I studied them, focused myself squarely on their texture, their weight, the tassels and...

"Howard."

I was lured from the curtains to the top of the stairs where Sylvia stood, waiting. The whispers that had grown louder as I studied the drapes immediately subsided, and as if they, too, waited for me to unlock Sylvia from the landing.

She was breathtaking. Her brown hair had been pinned, certainly by someone else, into soft curls atop her head. Her blue dress coaxed her eyes into a piercing shade of blue I never knew existed. Her Palter DeLiso shoes and matching purse had never been used, and I knew that a lot of thought and preparation when into that moment at the top of the stairs.

Beautiful, I said in a whisper, and she glided down the stairs, keeping her eyes on me as she carefully stepped with the new shoes. As she drew closer I saw that she wasn't wearing a trace of makeup, save a red, painted lip. I couldn't take my eyes off of them and Sylvia must have realized it because she delicately parted them and whispered, "Let's go, Howie."

It was a lot cooler outside than it was ten minutes prior. I offered her my arm and we walked a few block to catch the Seventy-One trolley car to downtown Pittsburgh. There wasn't an awkward moment between us, and the only quiet seconds came when she'd look away and I had an instant to take her all in. She acted like she didn't notice, but she blushed every time.

She crossed her legs at the ankles and held her bag on her lap. Even in 1937, a pair of new heeled-shoes and red painted lips opened up the evening to endless possibilities.

The Seventy-One dropped us off right in

front of the William Penn Hotel. Sylvia looked up at the impressive, opulent façade and let the breeze tingle her bare face. She had seen this place so many times, but confessed that no occasion had ever led her to the rooftop garden for dinner.

We were escorted to a table at the edge of the dance floor and she looked at me as if I had done something right. I was certain this was a scene from one of my movies. Orin Tucker and his band headlined that evening and his tunes carried on the breeze and, I was convinced, over the entire city of Pittsburgh. Bonnie Baker sang, "Oh Johnny How You Can Love," and I felt more sophisticated than I ever had in my twenty-three years. Elegant people dined at nearby tables, the cling of their wine glasses and the whirl of conversation sweeping us up into a giddy and intoxicated mood. "Oh Johnny" would only last a moment longer and I knew I'd have to say something right before it ended. I leaned in closer to Sylvia.

"What would you like to drink?" I asked, deepening my voice to perpetuate the maturity I felt running rampant inside me.

"I don't drink," Sylvia answered.

But now you're with me, I thought. Gary Cooper would never back down on a night like this. My voice got deeper.

"I'm going to fix something for you that you're not only going to like, but I promise, you'll want another."

She giggled, a soft sparkle in her blue eyes that made me dizzier. I ordered Benedictine and Brandy, and feigning all the sophistication in the world, I mixed the two and raised my glass to hers.

"Here's to you, Sylvia."

She sipped it slowly, indulging me. I could tell she was keeping it in her mouth and swallowing a drop at a time. But I didn't bring her there that night to show her what she had been missing in Benedictine and Brandy. I brought her under the Spring stars of 1937 to the rooftop garden of a restaurant that cost more than second-hand tires because my every intention was to propose marriage to the girl I had met on my brother's arm only months before. She cradled her drink in her hands, nursing it and sipping it so as not to dash my night of sophistication.

The busboys were clinging glasses and Sylvia spotted the saxophone cases coming out from behind the drums. We'd closed the place down. The Seventy-One took us back, and though the night had been exceptional and the few blocks to her house gave me more time to spend with her, I became distracted, lost in the composition of the sidewalk, in my brown loafers that I had worn at least a hundred times before.

"You all right, Howie?" Sylvia asked as she gently tugged on my arm.

"Fine, fine," I lied. I was drowning in stomach acid. I was now a block away and had thus far failed to do what I had come to Pittsburgh that evening to do.

"Here we are," she tugged again, luring me from my thoughts. It was evidently a very short block. The porch light was on but the windows were dark. She led me to the wooden swing and we sat. She folded her hands again on her lap and looked out into the dark street. I pushed off with my feet and the swing creaked with our movement. *Creak, creak, creak, creak...*

"Howie, did I leave you somewhere back there?" she smiled and I dropped my gaze from her crinkled blue eyes to her perfect red lips. I remember marveling at how they remained red the whole evening. And for some reason, right then, I started talking about my job, about a new set of animated films the studio was trying out called, of all things, *Looney Tunes* cartoons.

"I mean, what's a Looney Tune anyway, really?" I offered.

"Howie, there's a boy."

My throat closed.

"His name is Jack," she said calmly, coolly. I looked up from my shoes. She continued, "He wants to date me on a regular basis."

This wasn't possible. I had failed to account for any such thing as a *Jack*. I said nothing and she took it as a sign to continue.

"He thinks I'm something special."

I looked at her like she was speaking another language. I leaned in, even tilted my ear toward her as if I'd hear something entirely different from an unexpected echo. She folded her arms delicately against her lap. There. She had said it. And at that second I wondered if she, too, had wanted to tell me this all night.

This is what we called a pivotal situation in the sales field – the split second as the pen dangles over the contract, the moment before I'd have to bring out the big guns. This was one of those moments, perhaps the most important of my whole life. I locked my eyes on hers, possibly a little too fixedly because she blinked a few times

45

and slid back a bit.

"I'm sure he thinks you're fantastic, really I do, but if he knew the Sylvia that I know, he'd be here on this porch tonight and he'd be the one asking you to marry him." I almost didn't realize that I had said it. Her eyes began to pool.

"I spend a lot of time looking at perfect faces staring up at me from shiny pictures that I talk to day in and day out, the same perfect faces that are considered to be the most exquisite in the world. And it's my job to convince others that they can't live without them." I swallowed hard; I couldn't believe I was doing this. "I can't live without *your* exquisite face, Sylvia. I want to marry you."

I had thought out this moment so many times before, alone along the muddy creek beds. It was in me, a part of my makeup to play out both roles, to answer myself with a tearful embrace, but none of my fabulously concocted epics ended with the unmistakable clanging of glass bottles coming up the porch.

"'Evening," the milkman nodded, lugging his crate to the top of the steps. "You alright, Miss?"

Sylvia nodded as she blotted her eyes. Tears had fallen to the corners of her mouth and had pooled atop the brilliant red.

"Would you mind?" he motioned to the heavy bottles and we both motioned for him to proceed. He set them down.

"I guess you should be the first to know that I have asked Sylvia Shear to be my wife," I announced. She giggled and my heart began beating again. The milkman looked at her and she nodded confirmation.

"I've never run into this situation before, but I congratulate you both —"

I held up my hand. "Not yet. She hasn't answered me yet."

The milkman adjusted the crate on his hip and propped one foot on the top step. He was waiting, too. The swing creaked back and forth and the breeze brushed her face. She parted her ruby lips, and in a dreamy haze, Sylvia agreed to be my wife.

CHAPTER 5

I proposed in Spring of 1937 and on December nineteenth of that year I married Sylvia in a small ceremony in front of our families. The Rabbi blessed us and as we exchanged vows, I saw the most beautiful tear trickle down Sylvia's flawless cheek. Up until that moment I was a lucky young man, having found an unbelievable jewel in Sylvia, but it wasn't until that second, when I watched the tear drop from her face onto our joined hands, did the gravity of what we were doing hit me. And it really hit me. Did she know what she was getting into? I was a traveling salesman who just married a nice girl and who was about to introduce her to life on the road.

Our honeymoon began on a chilly train ride from Pittsburgh to Washington where I had arranged to pick up my car. We bundled ourselves in coats, Sylvia still wearing her simple and homemade wedding dress beneath hers. I caught her a few times during the trip studying her newly-banded finger, even placing it on the frosty train window, her palm melting the cold into the delicate silhouette of her hand.

It seemed that the weather warmed every mile we drove south on US Highway One on our way to Florida. The road was a long coastal vein that brushed the Eastern seaboard, so we took

advantage of exploring the little towns and quaint ocean-side stops. The most sobering thing crossed my mind somewhere in the Carolinas. I remember driving and watching Sylvia smile at seemingly nothing out the window and it hit me:
I'm responsible for her now.

I had driven a hundred thousand miles alone, never worrying about a passing truck, sharp turns or desolate highways. And now, here I was with a passenger, a passenger for the rest of my life and I sat up straighter and concentrated on the road.

"You okay, Howie?"

"Of course, darling," I said, my hands white-knuckled as I grasped more firmly on the wheel.

Somewhere in the Carolinas is also where Sylvia began shedding the clothes in which she had bundled herself. It seemed that in every southern state we crossed, she'd shed another article. By the time we reached South Florida, she was bare-shouldered in her camisole and coyly smiling at me with a mischievous glimmer in her eyes. I accused her of staging a striptease to run me off the road.

We stopped in Georgia for paper-shell pecans, and along with a cup of St. Augustine magic water, I got all the orange juice I could drink for a dime. I was intoxicated by it, and warming to the notion that I was now married, absolutely drunk off the possibilities of life with Sylvia.

The freedoms of life on the road as a movie salesman were, in part, as romanticized as the endless possibilities harbored by movies themselves. Those freedoms came with pitfalls like the requisite long hours, the thousands of lonely miles and making an office and home out of your backseat. I was a professional transient with a crisp white shirt and an official studio badge and not the sort of life that anyone plans for, especially not with a new bride in tow.

Sylvia knew about my life and about my dreams and I knew that I had in her a champion, a support system, a home. Her family was another thing, and it took many years of being coined the "the motion picture bum" by her father before I proved to him that my every intention was to make a life out of this *with* his daughter.

"What sort of man earns a living in the picture business?" he'd ask every time her mother asked about me.

And God love Sylvia, because like clockwork she'd always answer, "My Howie." She was blinded by the spontaneous and exciting side of my life and it was just a matter of time before she tasted the instability that conditioned the rest of it.

Conquering the movie business with me would test every ounce of her commitment to our marriage, and there were certainly times that I thought my choices had caused her to wish she had never laid eyes on Howard Minsky.

Just before the wedding I was transferred to Virginia, with my headquarters now in Washington, D.C. and my new territory covering Norfolk on the east, Bluefield, West Virginia on the west, and the Tennessee line again on the south. I had moved around before, but never with a wife. I was friends with the son of a prominent theater owner named Thalheimaer who also happened to own a Virginia department store and a good deal of real estate. In one of his buildings he had a tiny one-bedroom apartment he agreed to rent to us. Now that I had a $10 a week raise with the move to the Washington office, I could afford the $40 a month rent for the apartment. I felt very grown up now that I could really call myself a provider.

It was a lot of fun watching Sylvia set up our home and for the first time, begin to make her own decisions along with most of mine. She had grown up under the watchful eye of an Orthodox household. Moving to Virginia was not only a new beginning as husband and wife, but for her as a woman.

Up until that point, I had used my paycheck for bad diner food, new old tires, Evelyn's manicures and starchy white shirts. Sylvia restructured our finances and took the helm of a very tight ship.

I came home one day and noticed that envelopes were covering our tiny kitchen table which barely had enough room for plates and two sets of elbows.

"Ta-da!" Sylvia beamed like a pleased magician's assistant.

I scanned the envelopes and the perfectly written designations on each of them. This was my first taste of how things were changing.

"This one is for rent," she pointed out. I looked inside.

"It's empty."

"They all are," she smirked. She pointed to the others. "This one's for food."

I read them off. "Medicine, doctors, miscellaneous, recreation, entertainment, a dog... Sylvia, we don't have a dog."

"*Prepared*, Howard Minsky. We are prepared," she beamed. "As your checks come in, you give them to me and I divide them into these envelopes. Only if we have it in the appropriate envelope can we use it for that purpose."

"So if we run out of food money, does that mean that we eat the dog?" I asked straight-faced.

She giggled and shoved my arm as I shrugged my shoulders, teasing her and her envelopes.

We quickly became a fantastic duo in every sense. At home, when I was home, we were best friends; and in the field, Sylvia was my number one.

Shortly after we were married I bought a second-hand Underwood typewriter, I think for $29.00. It was a lot for us, but I had always wanted to submit my sales reports typewritten and clean. Sylvia had taken typing in school and liked the idea that I would recap my days to her as I dictated the meetings, negotiations and outcomes for the reports. She typed them for a number of years on the little Underwood. She'd work late into the night in the motel rooms we visited and sometimes, when necessary, she typed in the car, balancing the thing on her lap.

I wanted her with me. I wanted her company and her friendship and, I suppose, I wanted to show her off. There were cities and hotels I wanted her to experience and I knew that it wasn't easy being alone in Virginia, a newlywed and so far from anyone she knew.

We thought of other ways she could help me, and she devised what would end up being one of my strongest sales tactics. Oftentimes, I'd come across a reluctant theater owner or manager who just couldn't grasp the concept or the talent I was pitching. A lot of these men only spoke in dollars, and it took a little prodding to get them to see the possible return in my old black and white pictures.

I remember a few owners in particular; they wouldn't budge even though I told them that a new motion picture was gong to be the next big thing. They passed. Warner Bros. came out with a trilogy starring the famous Lane Sisters who were cast in the series, beginning in 1938 with *Four Daughters*, then *Four Wives* in 1939 and finally with *Four Mothers* in 1941. Priscilla, Rosemary and Lola Lane, along with Gale Page, played the Lemp sisters in the trilogy. It was bound to be a very popular series, and though I kept telling the theater owners why I thought so, I just couldn't get the contracts signed. Brilliantly, Sylvia helped me implement my very own form of PR. Like my early days trimming lettuce, I prettied up the picture so that it was irresistible. Our phone bills mounted, but the results were undeniable.

"Hello, excuse me, I was wondering when you are going to show *Four Daughters*?" she'd lower her voice on the phone and cover the mouthpiece to tell me whether they seemed to be biting.

"Shhh," I'd motion to her when she whispered to me mid-call. "They'll know it's us."

"Don't be ridiculous," she'd wave me off, and she'd assume another accent for the next call.

"*Hello*, yes, *hello*, I was hoping to see a film I've been hearing so much about. *Four Daughters*, when shall we expect it?"

It worked so well that Sylvia had my cousin call a few times, "for variety" Sylvia would say. Before I knew it I had contracts signed all over town. I'd end up relying on Sylvia quite a few times to wrap up some of the more difficult contracts.

It taught me another thing about pictures: creating interest in a property, the illusive buzz, was at the core of a picture's success. This would come in very handy later in my career.

"Don't get out of the car. Don't leave this automobile. Do not."

It had fallen on deaf ears before and I didn't know how to tell her delicately. Sylvia insisted on accompanying me on a particular trip and I was torn. I wanted her with me, but I knew that the place I was going wasn't any such place she should be.

"I *won't*," she sighed. She had heard me say it so many times before.

"I'm serious." I challenged her quiet smile.

"I know."

"Sylvia, I'm not kidding," I looked back at her as I made up the sidewalk with my book and a stack of papers. The Clinch Valley Theater where I had my meeting was a very old and neglected space, but compared to the rest of the small Kentucky town, it was habitable. When I got back to the car, it was empty. It took only fifteen minutes for me to finalize the contract, but that was enough time for Sylvia to wander from the car to the other side of the street. Clinch Valley was a sad place, almost as hard to look at as it was to live there. Sylvia was standing in the middle of the road, staring at a family that was passing on foot. With a backdrop of rundown storefronts and dilapidated homes, a young woman escorted her four children past us, all of them, except the youngest girl, averting their eyes. The little one smiled so big, and I could see that Sylvia wanted to smile back. She was distracted by the young mother who had lines in her face almost as deep and unforgiving as the mines that ran beneath us. Sylvia's eyes welled and she fought breaking down, for the little girl with lackluster hair was still smiling, craning her neck to stare as long as she could at my beautiful wife.

The car ride home was a quiet one, and our dinner together much the same. I was the one who was to protect her, and in some way, I felt like I had failed. New marriage is laden with these insecurities, but I managed to compound them with a lifestyle that Sylvia still struggled to understand.

CHAPTER 6

Shortly after the move to Virginia came another transfer to Buffalo, New York, one of the bigger cities serving motion pictures at the time. I was told that I was filling the position previously held by Burt Lancaster's uncle. He'd talk all the time about Burt and his aspirations to become a mainstream actor now that he was leaving the circus as an acrobat. I would cross paths with Burt Lancaster later in life and I always secretly pictured him in tights.

The move to Buffalo was an upward climb on the business ladder and a bitter taste of the uprooting to which Sylvia would have to grow numb for decades to come. We set up home in Rochester and I hit the theater circuit again, making sales calls and frequent overnight trips. I'd come home from work and Sylvia would show me one of the old pieces of furniture she'd found at a second-hand store and had hidden beneath one of her mother's linens. She made a home out of virtually nothing, and in my mind, it didn't lack a thing. She was hundreds of miles away from the only support system she had ever known and I was on the road four days out of the week. I was impressed by how she adapted to this new life with me, the "motion picture bum" who was, himself, insecure about all of the new changes.

I had married the most wonderful woman I had ever known, but at the core of my thoughts remained my responsibilities as a husband and provider. I'd excuse myself from the room when Sylvia would make her Sunday calls home to Pittsburgh and sometimes listen from outside the den door. She'd ask her mother and sisters about things I never knew were on her mind – ingredients in a recipe or how exactly she was supposed to wax wood furniture. Sylvia never once let on to me that she was overwhelmed or uncertain about being a new bride and wife. Rather, she had our home and lives in perfect order and made me feel like such a grown and deserving man, though I never told her that I sometimes still felt like a boy. I was still the youngest one out there, yet it now seemed less appropriate to remind me because suddenly I had the same responsibilities as everyone else.

I had to leave Sylvia for a few days in June 1940 to attend my first big Warner Bros. sales convention at the William Penn Hotel in Pittsburgh. It was required that we dress in our sales uniforms and that we "be on our best behavior" as the convention was helmed by none other than the Warner brothers themselves. Up until that point I had been throwing around the name Warner Bros. as if it was a title to one of my films or just the embossing on my official badge. Here I was in the meeting room of the William Penn, elbow-to-elbow with guys like me, staring up at the very men whose name I promoted as if it was my own. Being a part of the studio in 1940 felt like belonging to an exclusive club. Even though that room was filled with salesmen from other territories, I felt like I knew them. I had heard about their reputations and notorious tactics, sometimes their legendary antics. Though I looked like most of them, dressed and groomed and smiling the same way, I felt that sometimes I didn't quite belong there. My record on the road spoke for itself and my love for the job and for movies was unparalleled. But as I listened to their stories and reunions, I felt like maybe I *was* that "Kid" who lucked out in being there. Jack Warner broke my thoughts as he welcomed us to Pittsburgh and made light banter with his brothers. They each had a distinct personality, almost like a perfectly cast film of their own. Jack was the production chief, Albert was the treasurer, Sam the chief executive, and Harry was president of the company and the brains of the family.

"So I got on the train in Los Angeles and in my state room I found the most beautiful woman you've ever seen," Jack began and the salesman all locked eyes on him and his perfectly tailored suit. He was exceptionally well-spoken and held the room captive effortlessly, but you could tell that he thought the absolute world of himself. Jack playfully brandished his finger at us and made like he was staring the stunning starlet dead in the eye, "And I looked at her and said, Miss, I'm going to give you *three* days to get out of here." The room erupted with laughter and a peppering of catcalls. The men loved it and I laughed along with them so as not to seem like I didn't get it. I got it but didn't think it was all that funny. In fact, I heard Jack Benny quoted as saying that Jack Warner was a man who would rather tell a bad joke than make a good movie. His reputation was legendary, and so were his fights with his stars. I had heard about nasty rows with Cagney and Bette Davis, Olivia de Havilland and Bogart. But on that day, he threw out their names like confetti and made like there was no happier family than that of Warner Bros.

The Bros. each introduced themselves and then motioned to the back doors of the room where a handful of gorgeous actresses and actors entered and were escorted around the room. They were new players that the studio had signed, and what better way to make us feel as if we belonged with them than to trumpet them amongst us. The salesman often joked out on the road that we were the lifeblood of studio's web. Without the distribution we facilitated, the movies would stay in the can in Los Angeles. Only because of us did these flawless faces reach the backwoods and forgotten towns that many in Hollywood didn't even know existed. Feelings like this bred the notion that we were unknowns, blips on the radar of this all-important studio. We knew the famous faces only as much as we pretended to know them, only as well as our stories were believable. It was at this point during the convention that Jack Warner encouraged us to shake the hands of the actors — the moving versions of our black and white pictures. And in that moment, when the most lovely actress of the day looked into your eyes and read your name from your nametag, any salesman's cynicism became forgotten - at least until we were back on the road, wiping summer sweat from our brows, throwing out the names of people who didn't know we existed. I remember looking at the actors parading in front of me, wondering if I had, in fact, carried any of them under my arm, in my book.

The presentation fascinated me. Aside from the studio talent, who quickly left before our business commenced, we learned that the studio was planning to debut an animated rabbit named Bugs Bunny in a cartoon called *"The Wild Hare."* *Bugs Bunny?* I had never heard such a name. *How would I pitch a Bugs Bunny?* But I listened and apparently they were really excited about the expansion of their new franchise, carving out a place as the dominant studio in the 1940s in animated short subjects. That year we also had Bette Davis and Herbert Marshall in *The Letter*. Jack talked abut Errol Flynn, who was a big draw of ours in *The Adventures of Robin Hood* in 1938, one of the movies I had no trouble pitching to miners as a hero who could steal from the rich and give to the poor. It was secret vindication for them.

Much was discussed about another young actor who was developing a promising career with the studio, a short and unconventionally handsome guy named Humphrey Bogart. The next year he would be featured in Warner Bros.' *The Maltese Falcon* and in 1942 with Mary Astor in *Across The Pacific* and Ingrid Bergman in *Casablanca*. Little did I know at the time I was selling *Casablanca* what a place in film history it would carve. I had a very special connection to that film; it was co-written by a good friend of mine named Howard Koch. Howard was a real talent and a very good man. His professional fate would one day darken; he was fallaciously outed on the blacklist of presumed Communists.

Bogart became a favorite of mine, not just because selling him in a picture was guaranteed, but because he struck me as an everyman who had managed to emerge as someone really spectacular. Audiences loved him, and when he teamed up with Lauren Bacall in 1944's *To Have and Have Not*, and later in real life, they loved that even more.

I truly had one of the most exciting experiences of my young life being a part of that convention, and after getting over my initial insecurities, I felt like they wanted me there, that I was an important player in their very big picture. After all, they had to keep us happy, to get us eager to head back into our cars for the unforeseeable future and to make sure we left completely swept up in the infectious feeling of belonging. It was mission accomplished for me; I promised right there that I would go back out and do better than I ever had. It was a long trip home and I had a lot of time to think about what I had seen and experienced.

My mind raced during the drive. Though I tried not to confront it, one thing scared me, as it would any ambitious man trying to better himself and pave his own road. I, dressed in my requisite slacks and collared shirt, was not unlike the coal miners amongst whom I had been living for the past couple of years. For the first time I let myself think about the fact that I had grown up poor. I was never conscious of it in my ethnic neighborhood in West Philly. My friends were like me; all of our fathers were out of work. We played with Jews and Italians and Irish kids and we were all considered the same. I thought everybody was like us, and as I met more salesmen on the road, in these fancy grand hotels, laughing at sophisticated jokes, I could see more clearly how I fit into this world. I could now imagine what it was like the first time I walked into the miners' world and promised escapism and perfection as mirrored in my black and whites. That weekend in 1940, I, too, was staring at the images and taking in the stories promising proof that another world existed and was attainable for the most fortunate – for the hardest workers, for the most creative, for the undaunted and ambitious. I had made the same secret promises in the company of Jack Warner that the miners had made in the company of Howard Minsky and his grainy, Hollywood films: I was going to go out and conquer the world. Staring up at those celluloid promises, I know that the miners did the same.

After long trips or nights on the road I'd recap my stories and experiences to Sylvia at a very inexpensive Chinese restaurant we frequented in Buffalo. She was the best listener and gave me good advice, but most importantly, she wasn't afraid to tell me if I was wrong. I thought I was saying some pretty interesting things one evening when I noticed that she only responded by nodding politely. In a new marriage, your first inclination is that you've done something terribly wrong. Your second is that you're terribly boring. As she had assured me countless times that it was neither, I kept recounting a most frustrating exchange I had with the Buffalo office manager. Sylvia kept smiling and picking at her food, so I kept talking.

"Forty dollars a week. Can you believe that?" I didn't let her answer. "The senior executive in charge of my territory can't give me a raise because war is breaking out in Europe. *War!* So because the foreign market is so bad, I have to settle for my forty dollars a week or look for another job." I raised a cautionary finger to Sylvia who wasn't planning on interjecting. "And I'm not even considering another job." I picked up my fork and Sylvia reached out to touch my hand.

"I think it's a very good idea that you keep your job, Howie." I could see that she wanted to smile but didn't. I put down my fork.

"Howie." she lowered her voice and the busyness of the restaurant almost eclipsed her whisper. "I spoke with Doctor Burrows today." She leaned in and her eyes became glassy.

"Are you okay, Sylvia?"

"I think so. He told me that we're having a baby."

Holding my daughter Marcia for the first time was the most incredible feeling and the most frightening at the same time. The extent of my exposure to children was with Evy at the swing set when she came home covered in blood. And that hadn't gone as planned. I was now a father to a beautiful little girl who expected me to protect and know what was best for her, and I think Sylvia sensed my nervousness because she kept asking me if I was okay. It was hard enough leaving Sylvia when I was called away, but now I was leaving the both of them. I felt somewhat comfortable knowing that Sylvia would have

Marcia; the demands as a new mother would consume the hours that she used to say were unbearable when we were apart. I called home so often that the other guys would poke fun at me, but I didn't care. I had a wife and a daughter at home and Sylvia created another envelope for me to fill.

It was soon after Marcia was born that I announced to Sylvia that I had been transferred to Pittsburgh. It was bittersweet — she had tirelessly worked to set up our home in Buffalo, but Pittsburgh afforded her the family support that she had craved since we made our first move to Virginia. Though this would be our third move as Newlyweds, she began packing that night. I didn't let on that I knew just how excited she was.

The move to Pittsburgh came with a $10 a week raise and I felt quite good that I was moving in the right direction. Soon after settling in, we learned that we were having another baby and I became the father of a boy, Barry. It was an uncomplicated pregnancy and delivery, except for the theatrics in the delivery room of Mercy Hospital. I became severely ill, induced by nerves and by my mother-in-law. The hospital threatened to throw Sylvia's mother out of the delivery room because she refused to leave. The nurses sat me in a corner and monitored me as I watched Sylvia across the room. She didn't seem surprised that I was requiring more medical attention than she. We laughed about it later as we ate corned beef sandwiches and sour pickles, both sitting in her hospital bed, kids ourselves, now parents of two.

CHAPTER 7

The reality was that I had two children and was earning fifty dollars a week as a motion picture salesman. For my brothers, friends and many of the men I dealt with in business, the reality was Pearl Harbor and the draft. I was struggling to convince myself that my reality was, in fact, the same. I was a couple hours outside of Pittsburgh visiting a theater one afternoon and became physically and emotionally overwhelmed with what I was about to do.

I pulled the car into a parking space and sat there with my head in my hands talking to myself, trying to convince myself out loud that I would ruin everything good in my life if I went ahead with it. I slapped my cheeks as if I could strike the very thought from my head. I was watching the men in my life deploy to fulfill a purpose and duty to their country, while I spent my days only making up stories of bravery and honor.

I knew I was late getting home. I had been driving around town, minutes from the house, running the words over and over in my head. This was going to be the hardest sell of my life.

Sylvia was cradling Barry while Marcia played at her ankles. They were waiting for me on our hand-me-down couch, which we had inherited along with most of our furniture when we moved back to Pittsburgh. The house smelled of dinner, something with onions I remember distinctly, but I knew that the anxiety had eaten any appetite right from me.

"There he is! We missed you, Daddy." Sylvia sang as she lifted Barry toward me. I took a step back.

"Howard?"

She took Barry to her hip and studied me. I noticed that the table had been set with linens I had never seen before and pools of wax at the base of her grandmother's candlesticks reminded me that I had been driving around for far more than an hour. Sylvia followed my gaze to the table.

"I found them in the boxes. I swear Howard Minsky, if you make me move one more time before I unpack, we'll be living out of those boxes for the rest of our lives." She smiled and noticed that I hadn't.

"What's going on, Howie? She stroked Marcia's brown hair, knowing to distract her from the conversation.

"I stopped at the Naval procurement office today." I should have said nothing more, reversed the whole day somehow. I went on, feeling the need to explain.

"I told them that I was interested in the Navy." I watched her piercing blue eyes get muddy and for the first time fall gray.

"I passed the physical, but because I'm not a college graduate I can only be a Third Class Doorkeeper." I kept talking even though she was crying harder than I had ever seen her cry. A chilling, silent cry. Marcia looked up at her mother and didn't recognize her either.

"How?" she said, and though her voice was as soft as ever, the word cut me. "How could you do this without even discussing it with me? How could you come here and announce such a thing like it would be news to me Howard, like it was good news Howard! How!" She grabbed my face that I had turned away from her. "Look at me and tell me how." She had my chin in her small hand and I angled my eyes slightly to catch my son's face and my daughter now crying at Sylvia's feet.

"It's my duty," I offered weakly, though it was how I had felt for weeks.

"Your what?" she shot back. She motioned Barry toward me. "What, pray tell, is this duty here?" She wasn't crying anymore. She swallowed the tears pooled at her mouth and put the kids to bed. I didn't see her until morning. By then, the candles had lost all life, resting reformed over the newly discovered linens.

I was in the service for two years and my wife and children had to live with Sylvia's parents while I was away. I served in a branch of the Navy called the Seabees, also known as the U.S. Naval Construction Force. Our division specialized in maintaining infrastructures and staging areas for our forces. I was assigned to Camp Perry, Virginia where I would take basic training and then would be transferred to Davisville, Rhode Island. During the days I served in the Bureau of Supplies and Accounts as a physical trainer for commanders and flag officers, and at night I wrote letters home to Sylvia. It wasn't until I reread my scribbled hand on the cheap, military stationery that I was confronted in my own words by what I had done. Sylvia wrote back.

> *The kids were growing fast.*
> *Barry had taken his first step.*
> *Marcia was a chatterbox, precocious and bright.*
> *The house seemed different.*
> *She seemed different.*
> *Letter after letter, she was alone.*

I was alone, too, though the Seabees offered a camaraderie and a sense of belonging reminiscent of my early days on the road. But unlike the friendships forged with other salesmen, a cloud of uncertainty conditioned all military relationships. Movies offered the hope that one day, you'd work together again, perhaps a bigger role, a more important credit. The military, though enlisting you in a band of brothers, also presented the very sobering reality that friendships often lasted as long as you were stationed together, or during combat, as long as you kept yourself alive.

I'd tell Sylvia in my letters that I felt like I was part of something important. I told her that I thought about the nights we'd stay up late in bed, when the kids had finally fallen asleep, and talked about all of our big plans, all the things we'd hoped for. I told her that I still shared those moments with her in bed, only now I was hundreds of miles away and she was looking down at me from the tattered photograph I had taped to the underside of the bunk above. I told her that Teddy had come to visit me and that I got the biggest kick out of saluting my baby brother who had been discharged as a captain. I'd salute him and then quickly remind him of the bully with the mouse at the Hamilton School. I told her that I felt like I had again found the sidewalks of Robinson Street where I had once corralled the neighborhood kids into my productions. I had put together a show and cast my bunkmates, but there were no straight pins to be earned.

I told Sylvia everything – everything except that I blamed myself each and every night for leaving her when she needed me the most. It took me quite some time to say the words out loud and when I finally did two years later, she just looked at me and told me that she loved me.

I've always been a believer in good people. I've met my share of the other kind, but good people have always followed me throughout my life. Late one night in the barracks, one of the officers pulled me aside and handed me some paperwork.

I had been there almost six months, and when I wasn't working, I spent most of it by myself writing letters. A few times the officer struck up conversation with me, usually prompted by the newest photograph that Sylvia had sent in a letter. I told him about my family and about choosing to leave them. He'd listen to my stories, never really saying much. Finally, one night he asked me why I use such colorful words to describe the simplest things. I assumed he was referring to the way I told stories filmically. I was wrong.

"Howard, it's a lot simpler than that. Life isn't a movie. It's a whole lot simpler," he'd say.

At the time I didn't think he knew what he was talking about, until the next night when he handed me papers saying I was excused for a seventy-two hour leave from base. I tried to say something but he held up a hand and just repeated, "A lot simpler, Minsky." I later learned that he had lost his young bride while he was stationed away, and whether she died from a broken heart or not, he never really revealed.

I hitchhiked from Davisville, Rhode Island to Conneaut Lake, a summer vacation spot in Pennsylvania where Sylvia had taken the kids with her parents. I'd only have twenty-four hours to spend with them before I had to start hitchhiking back to base. I'd never hitchhiked before and it took me a while to get the hang of it. I was in uniform, which was an advantage when hailing a car, but a disadvantage, as I was exceptionally paranoid of being picked up by the shore patrol. I walked a good number of miles, the blistering pavement reflecting the sun into my face.

Our reunion was heartbreaking, as I knew the few hours I had to spend with Sylvia would ultimately end with my leaving again. Not only would I have to say goodbye, but I would force her to confront, all over again, the choice I had made on my own.

The two years in the service crept by. I was hospitalized with an injury to my left knee and following surgery, was medically discharged. On May 30, 1945, I left the Chelsea Naval Hospital and made my way home to Pittsburgh.

It wasn't the homecoming you'd see in movies with a tickertape parade and streamers hanging from the chandelier, next to a homemade banner in kids' finger paint. It wasn't the homecoming I had hoped for, but I suppose it was the homecoming I deserved. I was a stranger to all of them, and I couldn't blame them if they expected me to leave again by day's end. Sylvia had dressed Marcia in a sailor dress and she clung behind her mother's leg as she did the night I announced that I was leaving. Barry barely knew me, and often retreated into the other room, at times quite uncertain that he had ever seen me before. Other times, as the days passed, he was quite certain that he, himself, had enlisted with me and that we had just returned from a trip fighting the Russians. Sylvia tried to convince him otherwise, but he refused to let go of the idea that he was away at war with his father.

"This is daddy! This is daddy!" Sylvia cooed as she nudged Marcia into my lap, tugging Barry by the hand. "Go see daddy."

I smiled big and I think Sylvia knew I was fighting back a complete breakdown right there as my own children hid behind my wife.

The hardest part of returning home was reacquainting myself with Sylvia. I took it slowly, but it tore me apart to not be able to continue thinking and acting as we had before. We both grew up in those two years, but none of it together. As if I had just met her, I would begin to tell her about my life and what I saw and how wonderful I thought she was. She let me in immediately, but I knew that she was holding back a little bit of her heart in case I needed to leave it behind once again.

There was a chasm between my children and me. No matter how many photographs and stories we shared with them confirming my place in their lives, they needed their own time to sort through their very young memories and feelings.

Two nights after I got back, there was a terrible thunderstorm. Shards of lightning cut through the dark of the den and raindrops like angry fists pounded the roof. I was sitting alone in an old leather chair, listening to the most beautiful sound I had ever heard.

"Shhhh, it's okay," lingered from the depths of the coat closet. Whimpering and shrieks crept from under the closet door each time the thunder clapped. With each strike of lightening, Sylvia would calm the trembling voices escaping from behind the winter coats.

"Don't ever be afraid of thunder and lightening, she said melodically, and her voice carried over the raindrops. "That's God's music."

I sat in the dark, a stranger in my own home, and listened to God's music on the other side of my closet door.

CHAPTER 8

"It'll be okay, Sylvia, I promise." I hoped to God that my voice sounded convincing.

"But Howard, what are you going to do now? All that you've worked for," she said. I cleared my throat and spoke more forcefully as if it would convince the both of us.

"I'm going to New York and I'm going to align myself with another company. A better company."

I had just slammed down the phone after telling Jules Lepidus, the district manager in New York, to take his job and stuff it.

"Jules, you made a promise to me which you didn't keep. If I ever see you again you'd better walk on the other side of the street or I'll knock you on your ass," were my exact words. They are remarkably vivid some seventy years later. I had been promised the managership of the Buffalo office for years, and before I went into the Navy, it was mine. I was singled out by management as the one in line for the position, but as I learned that morning, a promise is only as good as the signed contract that comes with it.

Some years before I traveled in Kentucky and West Virginia, Uncle Harry saw potential in an automobile salesman named Benny Kalmonson and hired him as a film buyer in the Pittsburgh area. Benny's sharp tongue and sharper instincts allowed him to not only become an able film buyer, but ultimately helped him become the head of Warner Bros. motion picture distribution. He was a tough, tough guy and it was known that he didn't earn his place in the business because he was a sweetheart.

In my anger over being passed over for the promotion after coming out of the Navy, I may have said some things that crossed the line. In fact, I know I said some things that did. And I knew that Benny Kalmonson heard about it. From that point on, our relationship was strained, though my quitting was never brought up directly. When Warner Bros. acquired the distribution rights to *My Fair Lady* I had lunch with Razz Goldstein, the sales manager who offered me the job of supervising the distribution of the picture. It was a wonderful opportunity and I jumped at it. I was sobered soon after accepting the job, learning that Benny Kalmonson had learned of Razz's offer and vetoed the whole thing. He wouldn't hire me. Our relationship came to a head a few months later on a train from New York to Chicago.

It was a rainy night and the train was packed with tired commuters staring blankly out the windows or at wet newspapers. I was in the dining car and Benny passed me, putting his chubby hand on the table and leaning in with an invitation to his private compartment. I was surprised to be asked and went.

"Sit down, kid," was his opening line. "I want to talk to you." I knew then that this meeting was not to facilitate an apology or even a truce.

"I'm gonna tell you something that I wanted to tell you some time ago," he started and the room got smaller. "I never liked you and I want you to know that I never wanted you on my sales force. You're a fresh kid and I don't like fresh kids."

Well. I hesitated a moment and then uncorked.

"Benny, thank you for your frankness, and so, I'm going to be equally frank with you. I never liked tough guys. I never tolerated tough guys. And I may regret what I'm saying, but I never liked you either." I got up and walked out of his state room. I never again had occasion to meet or talk to Benny Kalmonson.

Sylvia placed one hand on my knee and her other one cradled her forehead. I wanted to come home from the service and get the job I had been counting on. I wanted a bigger paycheck to make proud the family that had put up with me, and now, I had just quit the only sure thing I had.

"It'll be fine. I promise you," I told her.

The next morning I headed to New York City and took meetings with various sales managers I knew at 20th Century Fox and Republic Pictures. It was a strange feeling entertaining employment from another studio; I had always associated myself with Warner Bros. The meetings were productive and almost immediately I was offered a position in New York with Fox. I was thrilled. It seemed so easy and I was in the mood to celebrate. I called my Uncle Harry, the most successful and level-minded man

I knew, and told him that I was in New York and had landed a fantastic job in the City. I walked into his office with a stupid grin, and before I could say a thing, he punched me in the jaw.

"Why are you such a smart ass? Tell me," he demanded as I felt my face.

I had never seen Uncle Harry this way. I felt a warm trickle from my lip and quickly licked it clean as if to hide proof that he had succeeded.

"What's the matter with you, kid?"

"They promised me Buffalo. I've been busting my back to get this job and they lied to me." Of course he already knew. No one knew more people than Uncle Harry; I was certain he got Benny Kalmonson's version of the story first thing today.

"Grow up, Howard. If you slam the door on every sonofabitch who disappoints you, you're going to end up in a room all by yourself. And then what are you gonna do? Make your own movies?" He studied me as I blotted my lip with my sleeve. "And that's no way to raise a family."

I told him about the meetings that morning and how Fox told me that there was a place for me with them. I wanted to bring the family back to New York. As I said the words, Harry dug deep into his pocket and pulled out a wallet thicker than his glasses. He peeled off a hundred dollar bill and held it out for me."

"Take it."

"What's that?"

"Your expenses for this ridiculous trip and the dry cleaning for the sleeve. Look at yourself, you're a mess."

"I want the job," I raised my voice and he

locked his eyes on mine.

"There is no job. When you get back with your wife and your children piled into that old jalopy, you will have uprooted everything for nothing, Howard. Where's your contract? Where's your big manager's advance for your moving costs? Hmm?" He challenged me, then brandished the hundred dollar bill in my face again. I turned away, rejecting them both.

"Come to the house tonight. Come have dinner with us and we'll discuss it." He put the money back into his pocket and cradled my shoulder.

"And clean up that lip before your auntie does the same to me."

Uncle Harry ran away from home when he was a little boy. I never knew why and he didn't talk about it, but whatever it was, he really didn't want to be found. He changed his name from Minsky to Kalmine after an acquaintance he met while living on the street. He found shelter in the Newsboys Home in New York City and stayed there until the war broke out.

In 1917, Harry enlisted in the military and served until he was shot in the head at the Argonne Forrest fight. He'd end up living the rest of his life with a metal plate in his head. He got a job at a new theater in Hackensack, New Jersey called the Oritani. At the time of its opening in 1922, it was being promoted as the new multi-million dollar Oritani. It was operated by a family of Greek brothers named Skouras who would end up becoming a big part of both Uncle Harry's and my life later on.

As a kid, I heard Uncle Harry tell these stories. They both fascinated and scared me – pretty much as he did. He was what every kid needed – an uncle who was two parts tough and hard-edged and the rest, benefactor and protector. Uncle Harry had earned a tremendous place working his way up in the business and ultimately became a prominent executive of the New York theater circuit. I admired him.

I had lived until this point as a salesman relying on instinct and intuition, honed by years of reading people and assessing their needs, wants and vulnerabilities. I had learned my customer service skills from the A&P grocery store and as a coat checker. With my lip throbbing, standing in that big office, I knew what Uncle Harry was trying to tell me, and he was right.

I stared at him over my aunt's roast beef, wondering as I had as a kid if he felt the metal plate inside his head and whether or not it would *CLINK* and *CLANK* if I tapped my butter knife at his temples.

"You are more ambitious that I was when I was your age, Howard," Uncle Harry tipped his wine glass in my direction, drawing me away from the patch of bald. I sipped my wine and it stung my open lip.

He continued, "You were right to slam that door Howard, but remember we have the same blood; I know what's in your head whether you like it or not."

Rather than answer, I swallowed mashed potato, hoping that he didn't know that I was still thinking about his skull. He waited.

"But Uncle Harry, there was a promise—"

"No buts, Howie. It was stupid. But I understand why you did it. I hope you've gotten this whole notion of upheld promises out of your system because you're going deeper into the trenches of show business and promises have no place in battle."

I watched him butter bread. He wasn't joking. He raised a sharp finger at me.

"And don't think I won't hit you for the very same thing again." He averted my aunt's glare.

Uncle Harry pulled out a piece of paper and a fancy pen and scribbled something down. He held it out for me.

"Go back to Fox tomorrow morning. There will be a job waiting for you," and he resumed the business with his bread.

I stared at the paper and deciphered Uncle Harry's unmistakable hand: *Tom Connors, Twentieth Century Fox.*

As Uncle Harry had scripted, the next morning I was sitting opposite Tom Connors, a big-timer at Fox. He was going over in detail my assignment to take over as manager of the Buffalo exchange. I was to go back to Pittsburgh and pack up my family. I wanted to tell him that I had to think about it, that Sylvia would have to make the decision with me, but the truth of the matter was that I had no job, two children and a wife that deserved an ounce of stability, even if it wasn't in the same place for more than a few months.

My stomach was in knots as I leaned over the pay phone, its metallic ring echoing through the dirty receiver. Sylvia picked up.

"Darling," my breathing was hurried.

"Howie?"

"Remember that cheap Chinese place we loved in Buffalo?" I lingered on the line as she took it in.

"Oh, Howard, not again. I just can't."

"Sylvia, remember my fifty dollars a week, honey, the fifty dollars I had to fight for?"

"Fifty is respectable Howard."

"How respectable is two hundred and fifty?" I held the receiver away from my ear as she screamed. Her voice echoed through the concrete alley.

"How do you like them apples!" I screamed with her. She was now laughing and I knew it would be okay. She'd put up with me one more time, have faith in the boy that promised to take care of her. I was doing the right thing; somehow I knew it.

CHAPTER 9

The move back to Buffalo was even more exhausting and chaotic than the others. More furniture, more boxes and another child. I had already assumed some of my duties, making phone calls and introducing myself to my sales teams and office staff. We settled into life in Buffalo quickly, having known the city helped more than we'd realized. Since the children were in school during the days and I was at the office, Sylvia had the house to herself and was able to settle us in seamlessly. I relished my role as manager and would come home recounting stories that even the children were beginning to understand. Sylvia laughed a lot more, more than I had seen since the carefree days I brought her into the depths of the mining towns.

Shortly after I started my position, I was invited to the New York City home of Andy Smith, sales manager at 20th Century Fox in charge of the Buffalo area. Over dinner and the usual pleasantries, Andy offered me the helm of the New York Exchange, one of the most demanding and prominent jobs for a manager. I wanted to say "yes" that second. An opportunity like this meant financial and professional accomplishment, but I could no longer make decisions hastily; I was no longer living out of my car. I had children at home who came home and told me that they liked school and liked playing in the yard. The boxes were finally unpacked. I owed it to all of them to hear what they had to say about a move to New York City.

Before I could muster the words to bring it up with Sylvia I received a telephone call from George Skouras, one of the prominent Skouras Brothers who were theater owners and moguls in the business. He and his brothers, Charles and Spyros, were a true rags-to-riches story. They were Greek immigrants and the children of a shepherd. They came to America in 1910 and sold newspapers and worked as busboys in a St. Louis hotel until they managed to save $4,000 to buy their first theater. They built an empire on saving their wages and pooling their efforts, and the three Skouras brothers ended up owning most of the theaters in St. Louis. An opportunity came in the late 1920s to sell their theaters to Warner Bros. and this branched each of them off into various parts of the picture business. They always stuck together, however, and in 1932 Charles, Spyros and George took control of over 500 Fox-West Coast Theaters. Even after running and owning some of the largest companies in motion pictures, Spyros kept his busboy apron in his office to remind him of where he came from and how he'd never let himself go back to that place.

George would eventually become the head of United Artists. I knew George from my many meetings in New York and had always admired his accomplishments and the stories that came with them. He called me that morning because he had a proposition for me. He was expecting a visit from a Greek war veteran who was coming through Buffalo and would need an escort from the train station at three o'clock in the morning. The veteran was a dignitary who was being honored at a very big assembly of the Greek community. They were arranging to send aid and supplies to Greece and a "who's who" would be attending.

I paced the cold, abandoned platform for an hour and a half since the train didn't bother coming in until 3:50 a.m. I was exhausted. I planned to welcome him, escort him to the hotel and be on my way. When the train rolled in and the passengers trickled off, I saw no sight of anyone looking for me, nor resembling the man I was sent to meet. Finally, when the platform was abandoned again, two men stepped down from one of the cars holding a third man. The third man greeted me with tired eyes, and I fought the urge to look down at his amputated leg.

I checked him into his hotel and stayed to help him organize. The veteran put away his belongings and I watched his right leg accomplish alone what most men required of two. Without looking back, he answered my silent question.

"It was shattered and they took it," he offered in broken English. Nothing more was said. I drove home that night wondering what life would be like if the tables had been turned and I had returned to my family as he had. My tired mind ran away from me and I thought about what Sylvia would have done if I hadn't come back at all.

I slept a couple of hours until George Skouras called to invite me to attend the war relief event that night. As tired as I was, of course, I accepted. That night I found myself in the company of dark-haired, dark-eyed strangers, and at first glance, I fit right in. There was a very warm and familial purpose to their activism. I watched as affluent and influential Greek-Americans mingled amongst war veterans and philanthropists. They moved mountains that night. I was thoroughly impressed by their plan to ship impregnated cattle to Greece, meaning essentially that their donation would multiply shortly after arrival. They arranged to send farm equipment, farmers who would share their methods and expertise, and of course, a lot of money. The evening was a big success and the presence of the visiting veteran was of great importance. For my part, I was rewarded with a handsome offer from George Skouras. He wanted me to come to New York and become an executive operating his family's theater circuit. I now had two offers on the table – take the helm of the New York exchange for 20th Century Fox and Andy Smith or become an executive in New York City with the Skouras Brothers.

The picture business was, and still is, a very small world, and somehow everyone and everything manage to intertwine. George Skouras ran his theater circuit and both of his brothers had a hand in it, but the oldest brother, Spyros, happened to be the president of 20th Century Fox and stayed at the helm for twenty years. After the Skouras' sold their St. Louis interests to Warner Bros. Spyros stayed aboard to manage all of Warners' exhibition houses. He went on to work for Paramount between 1930 and 1932 and then would leave to be the driving force behind saving the Fox Metropolitan Theater chain from folding. While at the head of Fox, Spyros bought the rights to the CinemaScope process, which at the time was the technology creating wide-screen, color epics. When you weighed both offers on my table, one with George and the theater circuit and the other with 20th Century Fox, I'd be answering to a Skouras either way you looked at it.

There was only one executive with whom I had to consult and she was at home putting the children to bed. I asked George for a few days and stayed up that night discussing the two options with Sylvia. She told me to stay put at Fox, reminded me that Uncle Kalmine had gone out on a limb and had opened a door for me at which I had been knocking for a long time. But the truth was that I wanted the prestige of the executive position with the Skouras'. I thought it was more prominent and that my title would open other doors for me down the road. I took the job and decided to leave Fox. Then days later, two top executives from Fox were killed in a plane crash. The industry was shaken up, as were my thoughts about my own vulnerability and how titles and executive positions meant nothing in the big picture. With the two jobs now vacant in Philadelphia, the Skouras' convened and decided that rather than coming to New York to work for them, I was to head to Philadelphia to run six exchanges for 20th Century Fox.

I would now oversee the administrative bodies of these six exchanges and facilitate the reporting back to the studio. The exchange would send out the movies and book the movies and we served as the arteries in the complex web of Fox's distribution. It was 1962 and I was making $500 a week. I remember seeing the first check and thinking I had come a long, long way from packing buckets of lard.

Amidst the instability at home, I was making professional strides, receiving calls from Hollywood players and being told that I was moving up at breakneck speed. I acknowledged and welcomed it all, but in the back of my mind I never forgot what Uncle Kalmine said about the trenches.

Our Germantown, Philadelphia row house with manicured lawns was a far cry from the back seat of the Oldsmobile and the Pineville Motel. And though I know Sylvia was wary about setting down stakes for the children, she eventually enrolled them in after-school activities and Hebrew school. I remember her once telling me that we'd enrolled in classes all over the Eastern Seaboard and that the kids had rarely finished one. Philadelphia would finally offer the stability that Sylvia and the children deserved.

From the outside looking in, it seemed like my rise in the business was a charmed one, with a seamless beginning granted by my Uncle. On the inside, we almost drowned in unpacked boxes, nameless schools and friends and the uncertainty and instability that were synonymous with the rewards. Though I had now defined my role within the entertainment industry, my children and wife were still trying to define their roles as my support system along with their own identities.

They were easing into this new lifestyle, picking me up at the airport and sharing my stories on the way home. Barry started a business shoveling snow and when he got too cold, Sylvia made me finish the jobs left up and down Vernon Road while Barry watched me from the window. Everything was perfect and stable, until Christmas.

Twentieth Century Fox had a policy of offering a Christmas bonus to employees based on the year's performance. News had spread at the office that everybody had qualified for the bonus that year and the morale coming off the announcement was infectious. While verifying the paperwork, I came across an accounting error that had double-billed the financials, reporting to New York twice what was actually brought in. I'd come to realize that the error was no accident at all. The numbers were inflated by false billing accomplishments put through by the manager of the Philadelphia office and the cashier. I checked and rechecked the data. No one was entitled to a bonus and it was up to me to break the news to everyone. It is at this crossroads in life that a man makes a decision that he knows, deep down, will sway his course. I pulled the report and decided, against my better judgment, that I would bring the error to the attention of the studio after the anticipated bonuses were paid. I fell victim to the enthusiasm of my staff, and I saw, as the money was paid out, that the good feeling began to spread to their sales efforts early into the next year. It was a fabulous motivator and my judgment was swayed as to how I should respond. However, the truth was that even I received the bonus, and it was all the more reason to bring what I found out into the open.

As the Philadelphia office exchanged New Year's wishes, I set off to New York to confront the issue. I told my bosses that I had discovered deceptive accounting practices and I was obliged to expose the manager and cashier for their fraud. New York called them in for the confrontation.

We were all in the same room and as quickly as I had explained my position, I was as quickly accused of knowing about and orchestrating the falsification the entire time. It became my word against the others. On the spot, I was fired. The truth fell on deaf ears and I had become the scapegoat. My tenure at 20th Century Fox was over.

I hit a professional low. Everything I had worked for for over twenty years had been thrown against the wall. I watched it slide down, slowly enough for me to overanalyze and second-guess every step that had brought me to that moment.

CHAPTER 10

"Listen to yourself, Howard, please," Sylvia begged for the twentieth time in half as many days. She was complaining that she didn't recognize me anymore, that I had become lost in my muddy thoughts, self-defeating criticism and, not to mention, the old bathrobe and beard I had hidden beneath. Others were ringing in the New Year and Sylvia reminded me under her breath that I should eventually get out and see the first month of it.

"Darling, this is a minor setback—"

I jumped on her words.

"Those crooks aren't setting me anywhere! I should have dealt with them right there when they were looking me in the eye."

"Howard," her voice was utterly beaten down. "Howie, look at me."

I reluctantly looked her in the face and it seemed like the first time in days.

"Do you trust me?"

She asked me this a lot. It was her way of bringing me back to Earth.

"Your worth as a man is not defined by a couple of lousy crooks and those who protect them," she said as she cradled my stubbly chin in her alabaster hands. "And if you let them, then maybe they're right about you. Hmm?" She waited for me to take it in. She let go of my face and backed out of the room as if to keep an eye on me, to keep me from falling back into the foreign trance of depression that I had never before known.

I started to see a therapist, something I had been conditioned to associate with outwardly crazy people. I remember thinking after the first few sessions, as the veil of intoxication lifted from me, that it wasn't the outwardly crazy people who were the ones to fear. Self-doubt and loss of self were silent and powerful killers that could take a man in their undertow when there was no sign of wake on the outside. It took a long time for me to rebuild my professional confidence.

I was at home reacquainting myself with my wife and children, and for the first time, saw the day-to-day required to run the household. Being a full-time father and husband allowed me to clear my head, and I realized that I had never taken a break to stop and enjoy who I was outside of my work.

It wasn't long after Paramount Pictures learned that I was no longer with Fox that they hired me as division manager in Philadelphia. I'd cover the same duties I previously held with Fox, but now for Paramount. I saw the opportunity as the first brick in rebuilding my professional confidence. It felt good to be back at work, but much of the blind trust I previously had with associates and colleagues was now veiled with slightly more skepticism and caution. I was tougher on myself, too. I didn't want to drop the ball or find myself in the same position again.

While managing in Philadelphia, George

Welter, an executive with Paramount in New York, toured our offices on an inspection. He stopped into my small space and asked me a few questions. He wasn't a big talker and I didn't suspect that he had formed an opinion of me either way. I told him what he wanted to know and then he left. I got a telephone call from him about a week later asking me to come to New York to meet with him. I was surprised; he must have gotten a lot more out of our brief meeting than I.

He asked me to become his assistant. He told me that I knew all the branch managers, all the men in the field and I could be a great help to him. He was a powerhouse in the company, in the industry, and it would have been foolish to decline. I took the job that day, but told him that I would be commuting into the City from Philadelphia. At least I wouldn't have to bring up another move at home. I began to commute to New York City from Philadelphia every day, catching the five a.m. train and trying to make the six o'clock out of the City at night. Eventually, the commute would take its toll on everyone. As a family we had to weigh our options, and we resolved to pick up and make new lives in New York. Sylvia took the helm of the family while I became George Weltner's liaison to Paramount's theater interests.

My job became faster in pace and more was expected of me. I wasn't only representing myself, rather, now my decisions and my actions spoke for the company and one of its top executives. I was delegated a lot of responsibility, though all wasn't so bad. Jerry Pickman was in charge of advertising and buzzed me one afternoon to let me know that John Wayne and Forrest Tucker were on their way into the office. This was a very new part of the business for me; up until this point I had made up all of my movie star conversations in my head.

I casually walked into Jerry's office, as if I was on my way to someplace else, and he introduced me as "George Weltner's guy Howard." I would have been "anyone's guy Howard" at that moment to be in the same room with John Wayne. He shook my hand and I nodded cordially, trying to mask how excited I really was. After all, how much emotion should a man really reveal to the Duke? He and Forrest Tucker had Jerry's crystal glasses full of whiskey and they weren't sipping them modestly. They were in good spirits, challenging one another as to who could drink who under the table. For a month I told everyone that John Wayne drank me under the table.

My job also meant entertaining and meeting George's colleagues from the West coast. It was during one particular encounter that Sylvia would cement in her mind the notion that, as long as we were in the movies, I belonged to everyone.

Barney Balaban, the then president of Paramount Pictures and his wife Tillie were to meet us at the 30th Street Rail Station in Philadelphia. We would join them that evening for the premiere of *To Catch A Thief* starring Cary Grant and hometown girl Grace Kelly. For that one night, the whole of Hollywood descended on my old backyard. Sylvia changed outfits about a dozen times, each time asking me how she looked, but ignoring whatever I said. All she kept echoing over my compliments were that Grace

Kelly would be in the same room with her that very night. I teased her, saying that if she were really making a fuss for Cary Grant, I wouldn't have blamed her at all. I have said that Hollywood and its lure give off a very potent and palpable euphoria. Even for those who've grown up in the business, who've seen the glitz and the glamour on the other side of the camera and the great PR machines, they are still curiously drawn in.

Barney and Tillie Balaban stuck out of the crowd like caricatures amongst the black and white of the station. He, in suit and tie, thick-rimmed glasses and a quick gait that led you to believe that he was someone on his way to somewhere important; Tillie, dripping in jewels, draped in silk and tip-toeing her high heels over the breaks in the platform. They were your quintessential power couple – he had all the power in Hollywood and she spent it.

Barney was movie history. He was born in Chicago in 1887 and grew up in the back of his parents' grocery store in the Maxwell Street area, playing hooky from his chores and visiting the Halsted Street nickelodeons. These stolen moments watching moving pictures and being around his Uncle Luzor, who was a musician in the Jewish neighborhood theaters, were Barney's first taste of show business. Paramount would eventually buy out the Chicago theaters that Barney would later own, and when the opportunity to helm the studio came at the request of Adolph Zukor, prior Paramount president and founder, Barney took over. It was said that Zukor wanted Barney, a tough, self-made man who wasn't afraid of a good confrontation, to be in charge to prevent the impending hostile takeover of the studio by Joseph Kennedy. Barney rescued Paramount from imminent bankruptcy.

From across the crowded platform, I pointed Barney and Tillie out to Sylvia, but I needn't have bothered. Sylvia's eyes followed Tillie as she navigated the crowd and the walkway, lifting her delicate hem and clutching a sparkling bag.

"Sylvia, close your mouth." I nudged her as I opened the door to greet them.

The studio head and his wife slid into the backseat of my blue Buick and Sylvia looked as if she was wondering if Tillie had ever been in a Buick. No sooner than I had pulled out of the parking spot, Tillie leaned over to her husband, fanning herself incessantly with her purse. Sylvia used the side mirror to watch her; Tillie's diamonds slurred into a blinding white blur as she moved her hand faster and faster.

"*Barney,*" her voice cut through the quiet. "This car has no air conditioning." Sylvia dared not to look at me.

"For crissake, Tillie, what the hell did you do before there was air conditioning?" he shot back. This time Sylvia looked at me.

Tillie slumped into her seat, fanning herself, a fine beading of perspiration above her perfectly painted lip.

I held Sylvia's hand as we crossed the sea of red carpet in front of the Translux Theater that Grace Kelly had set ablaze with flashbulbs a moment before. The future Princess of Monaco was on the arm of Cary Grant and they were perhaps two of the best looking people Sylvia and

I had ever seen.

It seemed that Tillie had her fair share of these evenings, for nothing seemed to peak her interest or so much as make her smile. We took our seat in the theater and immediately Tillie turned to Sylvia who was, up until this point, making a concerted effort not to look at her for too long.

"Care to join me?" Tillie motioned her bag to the back of the theater. Sylvia nodded, though she later confided in me that she feared something fierce being left alone with that woman. She'd tell me that the ladies room had as much energy as the red carpet, and she watched a line of perfect faces blot and dab themselves silly, smoking long cigarettes and not caring all that much that the movie was about to start.

Tillie leaned into the mirror and watched Sylvia from the corner of her eye, seemingly reading my wife's thoughts as she studied the row of flawless women.

"Barney has a mistress you know," Tillie spoke as if they were the only two in the room. Tillie checked her perfectly penciled brows as Sylvia averted her eyes. What could she possibly say back? Tillie turned to Sylvia.

"You want to know who the mistress is?" she challenged Sylvia who was unknowingly clutching her purse to her chest. Tillie let out a long, deep breath as if she had been holding it in forever.

"The bitch is Paramount Pictures."

CHAPTER 11

New York City, herself, was a fabulous character in our lives. We never had so much fun exploring neighborhoods and landmarks, feeling like such a part of a very wonderful place. Philadelphia was our home and our children finally found some normalcy there, but New York is where Sylvia and I grew up together.

One night we were out with Barry and we stopped to get a pizza. We crammed into the elevator with a very good-looking man wearing makeup. He was staring at the pizza box and addressed us in the most upper-crust English accent, punctuated by a trace of Scotch.

"Would you mind terribly if I had a bite. I'm ravenous when I finish a show."

It was Richard Burton. He was just coming off of a performance of *Camelot* with Julie Andrews. Barry propped the box lid open in the elevator and Burton tore a slice, dripping with cheese. He chewed as Sylvia exchanged pleasantries. I'd meet him years later when I became an agent, trying to court him into representation in Rome. He was visiting his wife Elizabeth Taylor on a film. I'll never forget, it was early, early morning and Burton started it off courting a Bloody Mary. He offered and I declined, not possibly imagining Vodka before eight a.m. I reminded him of our first meeting in the elevator with the cheese pizza, and he sat back, closed his eyes, and as if recalling the most exquisite image, told me the way you'd imagine Richard Burton would while in Rome, that it was exceptional pizza.

And then some people get reputations as drunks and don't really deserve it. We were with Paramount people in Atlantic City and we went to Skinny D'Amato's to show our support for Dean Martin and Jerry Lewis who were headlining. They were doing their classic films together under the Hal Wallace banner and Paramount was very keen in those days on supporting their players. We took a table and watched them do their magic, the audience completely enthralled. I had heard a lot about both of them, but if anyone knew not to believe what you read, it should have been me. Dean was branded as a drunk and it fit into his act on stage as the womanizing, ultra-suave counterpart to Jerry's bumbling softy. Reality couldn't have been more contradictory. Dean was the nicest guy a person could want to meet. He was very hospitable and appreciative of his fans and of the fact that we came in for the show that night. Jerry wasn't the light character he brilliantly portrayed in his act. We were told that he didn't have time for us and that impromptu meetings like ours annoyed him. Dean was a diplomat and smiled his trademark, good-looking grin – the one where his eyes crinkle at the corners. He apologized for Jerry and said he was probably exhausted, a victim of their schedules.

It took a long time, but I eventually learned

that falling in love with someone on screen is perfectly okay as long as you never meet the person in real life. The script you imagine for them is always better than what they could possibly say on their own. You're almost guaranteed to be disappointed.

The life of an assistant is short-lived, but it's a crash course in many things useful. As Weltner's right hand I was privy to another world within the studio, understanding the business nuances and bureaucracy that life on the road and in cities outside of corporate Paramount didn't expose. When my tenure as an assistant was up, I was promoted from within to supervise Telemeter, Paramount's pay television outfit, on the sales level. Pay TV was a relatively new and developing concept at the time. For a few years I stayed with Telemeter and would spend a great deal of time in Etobiko, a suburb of Toronto, Canada. The studio owned a company there called Famous Players, and we had set up a test area where I would monitor and oversee Paramount's developing interests. I didn't realize it then, but I was being watched closely by executives from other companies. Just when I thought that I had traded in motion pictures for television, I was courted by one of the business' largest screen concepts called Cinerama. Cinerama exploded onto the scene as a direct response to the growing popularity of television. Theaters needed to pack a bigger punch, to make the movie-going experience worth leaving home for again. Cinerama promised that and more by introducing a technology invented by Fred Waller in the 1930s but that didn't become public until 1952. The idea was to synchronize three projectors with images cast on a 146-degree wraparound louvered screen that made you feel like you were sitting *in* the film. It was an incredible time in movies. I was made an offer to join Cinerama at the height of its growth. I didn't want to leave Paramount, a company that was full of people who were good to me, but I couldn't turn down the move three rungs up such an innovative ladder. I worked hard at Cinerama, traveled the world for them, and within a year, I was Executive Vice President of the company.

The head of Cinerama was a man called Nicholas Reisini. Reisini was a Russian who had come to the Untied States by way of China. His earliest contact in America was with the hierarchy of the Greek Orthodox Church, and to the public, Nicholas Reisini was a Greek. He was an import/export tycoon who had taken over at Cinerama with real vision for aggressive global growth. He wanted to take the technology to the countrysides of Europe where no theater could be accessed, yet untouched by Hollywood. He'd have a tent constructed and would have thousands of people watching a Cinerama film. He stressed the importance of content and made a shrewd deal with MGM to produce a string of films that he knew would work in his format like *How The West Was Won*, *The Wonderful World of the Brothers Grimm*, and *It's A Mad Mad Mad Mad World*. Nicholas Reisini was a sharp and brilliant businessman who took me under his wing immediately. I became very close to him, and I sensed, without a doubt, that the relationship was mutual. I felt very comfortable around him, and I recall thinking on many occasions that I was very lucky to have found, within this business, a sponsor like Uncle Harry and a mentor like Nicholas Reisini. Reisini pushed me to recognize my strengths and talents and motivated me to move up within the ranks of Cinerama.

My duties for the company required me to report to the money people and the money people included Bill Forman, a very prominent California theater owner. Because it was Forman who placed me with Reisini, I felt an allegiance to him, an unspoken responsibility to keep him in the loop as to what was happening within Cinerama. Though siphoning information to Forman made me really uncomfortable, he was asking me for it. I found myself reluctantly trying to appease two very powerful masters. I felt like a spy.

Cinerama allowed me to regain the momentum of which I lost sight at the end of my tenure with 20th Century Fox. I was more aware of the dynamics around me, almost as conscious of the people who ran the business as I was the company itself. I never wanted to be in the same position again, at the mercy of others, when I myself could have prevented it. Knowing this, I struggled to keep my allegiance to Bill Forman.

As the kids grew up, Marcia off to college and Barry in prep school, Sylvia and I took up as a team again. Though we didn't have the $29 Underwood typewriter in the car with us, we were again inseparable. I would travel the world for Cinerama, meeting, courting and negotiating with international screen interests, and most of the time, I had Sylvia protecting and supporting me as I did it.

I'll never forget taking her to Japan. I was called there to secure monies that were owed to Cinerama. Arrangements had been made for us to meet Cinerama associates from Nagoya and Tokyo for an evening in our honor at one of Japan's most intriguing and misunderstood venues – a Geisha house.

Sylvia started the day in our suite at the Akura Hotel with two elegant Japanese women who had come to demonstrate the fine art of traditional flower arrangement. The women set out before Sylvia, almost ritualistically, flowers and foliage that she had never before seen. Each movement seemed laden with meaning. Delicately, they cradled and moved with each stalk, each stem and flower with ceremonial grace. I was making phone calls in the next room at a desk propped in front of glass wall overlooking the city. I peeked over to see Sylvia awestruck. I never imagined that, by the end of the night, she'd be undressed in the bathroom of a Geisha house.

To an outsider, the Geisha are shrouded in an exotic veil of intrigue. With lacquered, porcelain faces and delicate soft-spoken voices, the Geisha are trained from an early age to become the most consummate hostesses. They are trained in art, music, dance and etiquette. They are educated in secular and traditional customs and can maintain a spirited conversation as readily as they could giggle at the most provocative discussions, so as not to offend their guest. Ritual and elegance was the way of the Geisha, but just as the Westerner looked in wide-eyed and curious, the Geisha stared back with the same curiosity.

It was the most elegant of dinners, one I later heard cost over $50,000 for no more than twenty guests. We were in awe of the attention paid to each of us, as an assigned Geisha doted on our every comfort. They were our escorts, our entertainers, our diplomats and hostesses.

Sylvia, the only female guest in the room, excused herself during dinner to the ladies room. At once, all eight Geisha rose from their knelt positions and followed her with tiny staccato strides.

Sylvia would tell me the story in vivid detail. The nine women exchanged quiet and kind glances as Sylvia made her way into the restroom. When she came out, the Geisha all watched. For most women this might be disconcerting, but for Sylvia, it was intriguing.

A young Geisha with cherry-red lacquered lips boldly motioned to Sylvia's hemline. Sylvia followed the young girl's fingers to the bottom of her dress. The other Geisha nodded agreement; they wanted to see what Sylvia was wearing underneath.

Sylvia took a deep breath. They told her that they wanted to see her underwear, to inspect her bra and touch the fabrics. Sylvia did exactly as they requested. They ran their tiny white hands along her clothing, giggling each time they touched Sylvia's skin.

She later told me it was one of the most unusual experiences she had ever lived, but as odd as it may have been, said it was truly nothing more than women discussing women's things.

"Weren't you embarrassed?" I marveled, intrigued myself. I was in absolute shock. No such thing happens in the men's room. Sylvia's eyes softened, her own perfect lips curling into a soft and knowing smile.

"Not at all, Howie. They were as curious as I was. They wanted to know the materials under my clothes, see how I wore them, how they fit. They wanted to marvel at the differences between my silks and lace and their very own." I couldn't believe it. I had never heard of such a thing; I don't think I could have made it up even on my best day on the road.

"They got me undressed, studied me and then helped me into my clothes, delicately, as if they had imparted their ritual upon me. Japanese or American, it made little difference when we were all standing there in our underwear."

I wanted to always protect her and I suppose there were a lot of things in our lives that were out of my control. Moving to the South and traveling through new towns right after we were married was both exhilarating and eye-opening for her. I had been conditioned to understand that people are products of their environments, upbringings and social boundaries. Sylvia had been sheltered, and life often surprised her.

We were still kids when I took her on a trip to see one of my very good clients in Virginia. I insisted we stop at the Roanoke Hotel, which was a railroad hotel that had a fine restaurant known in those parts. We met a dear Philadelphia friend of mine in Roanoke by the name of Al Mamlin. Al was a salesman for a fizzy drink that had just come out called Dr. Pepper. I had no idea what a Dr. Pepper was, but he said it was very popular in the South and that he was doing quite well for himself selling it out on the road. I had to make a one day trip outside of Roanoke and rather than dragging Sylvia along with me, Al offered to entertain her for the day. I knew she loved to swim and the weather was perfect for it. He said he knew of a swimming pool and that he'd escort her there the next morning. Sylvia wore an old bathing suit that she never had a chance to use. Al took her to the gate of the pool, and at the entrance a sign read, "No Jews Or Dogs Allowed."

Sylvia stood there and stared, the laughter and splashing of young children filtering through the iron bars. Her eyes welled but she refused to let them break. She later told me that she had never seen anything like that and I reminded her that the South in the 1940s was a very different place altogether. She finally broke down and cried, telling me that the sign looked custom made. She asked me through her tears if I thought any such sign-maker could really exist.

I didn't have Sylvia with me during my meeting with Jimmy Hoffa. Sylvia and I had just arrived in Aruba for a much-needed vacation and we had convinced ourselves that absolutely nothing would ruin that trip. No sooner than we had made the pact and sipped something ridiculously sweet and tropical, I received a telegram from Cinerama. I was needed immediately in Chicago to take a meeting with Hoffa, Teamsters president. It wasn't a trip Sylvia needed to make with me, as I knew that Hoffa was deep in the middle of a jury tampering trial and that my access to him would be at odd hours and in the middle of a potential publicity frenzy. My job was to ask Hoffa for a three million dollar loan.

It sounds a lot more intriguing than it really was. There was no underworld liaison, no secret meeting. I was surprised to find that the man that the media had portrayed as a one-dimensional thug was, in fact, exceptionally sharp and articulate. He rendered me speechless, though I never let on. I watched him compute strands of numbers I threw at him, numbers that our entire team of accountants crunched ahead of time. He was brilliant. I had heard that his father was a coal miner and died when Jimmy was only seven. He and his mother were alone and he dropped out of school at fourteen to look for work in Detroit to help support them both. Of course, I never brought it up, but the abandoned son of the coal miner had no idea just how much of his world I understood. In a way, I grasped his preoccupation and allegiance to a unionized way of life, to control and regulations, to the checks and balances that I never saw in 1930s mining life. I should have told him about the time the Union threatened to blow up my motel, but on second thought, perhaps it was best I didn't.

More and more, at times that I had to travel, Sylvia asked me if she could just stay home. I didn't understand why, but I assumed that our new lifestyle had caught up to her. I was seeing changes in her, lows and highs that I dismissed as fatigue or as her just being overwhelmed with the pace of our lives. The children were old enough to notice her swings, too, and for some time,

Sylvia passed it off as everything from menopause to lingering thoughts of losing her children as they grew up and went away to start their own lives. Deep down I knew it was something more. Her moods began to manifest themselves as entire days of total isolation, or at the extreme, binges of compulsive eating or shopping. I later learned that she had fought to suppress symptoms since our earliest years in Philadelphia, and now, they started to engulf her. While I was at Cinerama Sylvia was diagnosed with manic depression.

One can image the thoughts and insecurities that ran rampant in my head. The one person I promised to protect had been spiraling for years into absolute helplessness and I didn't do a thing about it. I moved us from city to city, town to town. I promised stability and assurances, and late at night, when I was alone in my thoughts, I wondered if the ups and downs in my own life manifested themselves in hers.

Doctors told me that she was incurable, that the deterioration would compound and that I was to provide a safe home for her and accept mania in our lives.

Sylvia spent seventeen years in and out of hospitals. Pills and needles and exams and false hope; we had grown accustomed to all of it. With her ebbs and tides, I rode the seventeen years as if I was put on the Earth for no other reason. This was a woman who earned her Ph.D. in redefining house and home because of me; the least I could do was to be the one constant in this time of complete uncertainty for us all. I owed her at least that much.

Marcia and Barry didn't understand what was happening to their mother, and slowly, as the illness ate away at Sylvia's happiest days, it also took a part of the family. It was Sylvia, who in these times of crisis, would take the household by the reigns and bring everyone out of the depression. Now *I* was knee-deep in the darkness and faced holding together our children and rehabilitating the very crutch that I had always expected to be there. I drew a strange parallel between this period of our lives and the years I spent in the Navy, with Sylvia never really knowing my fate or whether I'd ever return. Now, I did the same. Day in and day out, even though she was lying next to me, I wondered if she'd ever come back. She was no more whole or real than the tattered photograph I had taped to the barrack bunk.

Imagine seventeen years with your eyes closed. Imagine wondering if in the next moment your spirits would plummet so low, that you'd do anything to hide beneath them and never surface again. Imagine being so scared when you finally felt happy, because you knew, within seconds, you could be stripped of any memory of what that happiness felt like. This was Sylvia's seventeen years. Her eyes were closed to the changing lives around her – our children were maturing, developing their own identities, accepting admissions to top universities, and wondering if they'd ever know their mother in the same way again.

Hope came in the form of Dr. Theodore Rich, a California physician who tirelessly studied Sylvia's symptoms and researched possible treatments. The government had only permitted certain physicians to medicate with lithium as a mood stabilizer, and it wouldn't be approved by the FDA until 1970. With a pharmacologist at the Veteran's Hospital, Dr. Rich began treating Sylvia's manic depression with lithium. I swear, the very day he gave it to her the crippling fog lifted. For the fist time in a long time, I saw traces of my wife that I secretly feared were gone forever.

Without the pills, a bad day meant operating on severe highs, levels that would send Sylvia to the store to return with fifteen pairs of shoes. In a hyper state, I would watch her abandon all normalcy and caution and self-medicate with the most extreme behavior.

Like any woman balancing household, husband and family, Sylvia had her insecurities and fears. I blamed myself for not seeing them, recognizing them as more than life's everyday anxieties, and for somehow not being able to quiet them before they started to take her away. The early effects of the illness slowly crept into our storybook life while Sylvia blended the family into the suburban Philadelphia landscape. The children were then in school, Marcia at Girls High and Barry at the Cheshire Academy. I was away most of the time, working at full capacity. Sylvia would sit at home, staring at herself and her belongings as a stranger would, never knowing at the time that the emotional swings she was suppressing were beating her numb. Everyday life seemed to continue without Sylvia; she feigned interest in everyday pleasures for the sake of her family, and in return, we feigned ignorance to the chemical monster slowly suffocating her.

I knew how important it was that the children understand that their mother's struggle wasn't to be a hidden or shameful period. The truth was impossible to keep from them, especially after one very late night in Philadelphia when I had to call the psychiatrist to the house. Sylvia was trapped in a terrible emotional tailspin. I paced at the foot of our bed as she cried, clutching her face in her hands so that no one could see her. Marcia stood in the doorway, watching the doctor who had run up the stairs flash a light in her mother's blank, lost eyes.

"What's happening?" Marcia asked.

I never answered the children, because at that time I, myself, didn't know what was happening. That night Sylvia was rushed to the hospital, the way so many nights would ultimately end.

Though Marcia and I saw it creep up over time, Barry was away at school. His visits were far enough apart to really shock him when he was face-to-face with Sylvia, confronted with his mother's physical and emotional deterioration. When Sylvia was diagnosed in California and subsequently admitted for observation and treatment, I included the children in the hospital visits and consultations. I kept them informed whether the news was good or bad. It was the only way that we could conquer this as a family. Sylvia moved into a private hospital and found herself in the company of many intriguing and talented people – famous actors and artists whose creative lives had also somehow managed to change from color into black and white.

The kids would often ask me why mother

was sick, wondered what it was that sent all of us so far off course. I never told them because I didn't really know, but I often wondered if the onset of her rapid deterioration could be traced to one particular episode. Sylvia had a horrible argument with her father just before she slipped into this world of her own. Could it have been the breaking point of a lifetime of being controlled by him? I became used to seeing faint changes in her with every strained interaction, but I never imagined that any father-daughter tension could manifest itself in this way. Their last episode could have been the turning point, but again, I'm grasping for answers. After that exchange, she never was the same, and though I never mentioned it, I trusted that the deep, unresolved issues stemming from her upbringing plagued Sylvia far beneath her porcelain skin.

What was happening at home was hard to keep out of my professional life. I was not only traveling for Cinerama but was visiting California frequently for Sylvia's medical attention. Bill Forman approached me one day and offered some advice which would fly directly back at him a million miles an hour. While Sylvia was battling the dizzying highs and lows of her disease, he would negotiate his last deal with me. Bill looked me in the eyes over his large, shiny desk and leaned in.

"Divorce her," he said in a low voice even though we were the only two in the room. He tilted his furrowed brow slightly, as if letting the whole plan slide from his twisted brain across the blotter to mine.

"Get rid of this problem," he said definitively.

I looked down at my hands clenched in my lap. I hadn't slept much the night before, and as if Forman knew, he sighed.

"I'll run interference and handle the details. I'll have it done on paper before you even have to tell her. You don't have to live like this. Look at you."

The words rattled in my head; it was clear what Bill wanted me to do.

"I'll get a divorce," I locked my eyes on Forman, who leaned back in his big leather chair.

"That's the Howard that knows what he wants," Forman said as he motioned to put his finger on the intercom buzzer. I stood and held up a finger, cautioning him to stop. My finger slowly angled until it was pointing right back at him.

"I'm divorcing *you*. Run interference on that."

With that, I left my Executive Vice President position at Cinerama right there in the lap of Bill Forman.

He wanted me to abandon Sylvia while her eyes were closing, leaving her to ride the crashing waves of mental illness alone. There was no way in hell.

The whole episode brought again to the forefront something that I not only saw on the road as a kid, but by the end of my almost seventy years in movies, that I knew to be true – the frailty of the distorted Hollywood marriage. Though I've met a few couples that shatter this generalization,

I will stick to it, and being a man in my nineties, you'll bear with me. Marriage in Hollywood, as I knew it, wasn't an institution or a sacrament to uphold, aspire to, or protect. Rather, it was the fodder for good publicity, the thorn in an otherwise perfect production schedule, and an impossibly insatiable monster which required too much time, attention and effort – all which were better redirected into getting ahead. It's impossible to put your spouse ahead of you if *you* are the center of the universe.

I'm not throwing a blanket over the entire industry as anti-marriage, and yes, pressures at work do infiltrate non-Hollywood marriages, but in no other business does being married seem to count as a strike against you. I remember I was just transferred to a head office in Washington, D.C. and I'll never forget Fred Biersdorf, my new boss. When I met him for the first time I was a newlywed.

"So I understand you just got married," he cut to the chase, bouncing his beady eyes from my silly grin and Honeymoon tan to my simple gold band.

"Yes, sir," I answered. He shook his head as if he had just received a very sad telegram.

"You're not going to be able to fight back, Minsky. You're married and married men just can't fight back." It was so matter-of-fact for him.

"Who am I fighting back, sir?"

"You're a Junior salesman, kid. If you want Senior, you're going to have to want it, really want it and fight for it. But you have responsibilities now. You're not out there alone anymore, and you can't put it all on the line if you're worried about how it will trickle back to the missis."

I dismissed what he said at twenty-four years old, but I'd think about it and come to see it over and over again in my life. I'd face it in that office with Bill Forman who was more than happy to run interference for me. When I was an agent, temptation was ever-present. My job meant that I would be surrounded by gorgeous starlets who wanted my undivided attention, and it wasn't because I was a nice guy with a knack for engaging conversation. Around me, in front of me, colleagues and acquaintances traded spouses, homes and lives, and this was altogether okay. I've heard the counterpoint, too – non-Hollywood marriages break up all the time, we just don't hear about it. Sure they do, but they aren't often entered into because your agent and publicist think it's a good idea.

So I quit Cinerama and was again without a job, this time at my own hand. The old Howard would have relied on Sylvia to break him out of the impending rut, but things were now different. Sylvia needed *me* now.

One thing I always did, and still do, is keep in touch with those people in my life who have made it worth living. In a business such as mine most of the faces and names are worth forgetting, but there are always a select few who deserve knowing that they helped change your life in indescribable ways. I have always been lucky in meeting people who have launched my career and life on courses that I had never imagined possible. One of those people was a former employee of Bill Forman's, a man by the name of Benny Thau.

Benny was a senior executive at MGM who

was a powerhouse in casting. When Metro changed hands and Louis B. Mayer was no longer there, Bill Forman offered Benny a job and, I'll never forget, a new car as incentive. We became good friends at Cinerama, but it wasn't long after he was courted that he was fired by Forman. That should have been an indicator to me that Bill didn't recognize the best people he had, nor how to keep them. Benny and I grew close. He knew about my family and my responsibilities at home with Sylvia. Word came around that I quit Cinerama and he was the first person to call me with an option.

"I want you to talk to a friend, Howard," Benny insisted. "His name is Abe Lastfogel. He's the head of William Morris."

I knew William Morris well. Who didn't? It was the top talent agency in the industry and launched the format for today's mega-machines of talent representation. I had never entertained the agency world, but as Benny reminded me, it was all sales in different clothing. I agreed, and Benny made the arrangement. I flew to Los Angeles.

My kids, Barry and Marcia, always watching
over my shoulder in everything I did

President of Paramount Pictures,
Barney Balaban, and his elegant wife Tillie

Meeting the Queen Mother at the
Command Performance of Love Story in London

On the road for Cinerama with Sylvia in Japan

One of the greatest mentors I've known – Adolph Zukor, founder and longtime Chairman of Paramount Pictures

Brandon De Wilde sitting at my desk:
He stole the screen in Shane opposite Alan Ladd

A meeting with Jack Palance

Me and Johnny Carson

The Love of My Life

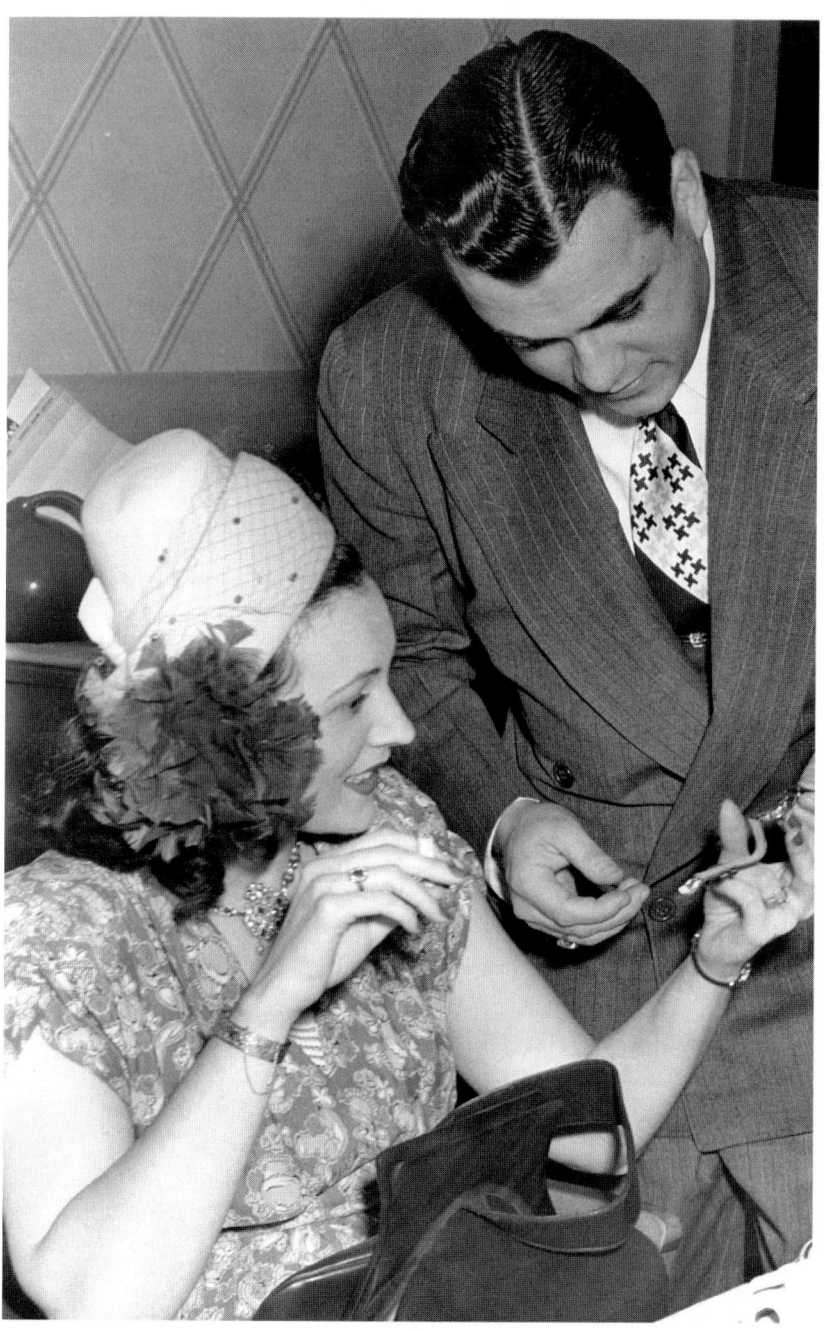

With my own leading lady, Sylvia

My mom and dad

My siblings. From L to R: Me, Joe, Evelyn and Teddy

Sylvia and I in the park with daughter Marcia

My family on the road – the other Warner Bros. salesmen

The Warner Bros. sales convention at the William Penn Hotel, Pittsburgh, June 1940. I'm in the fourth row, aisle seat

CHAPTER 12

Of the thousands of meetings one takes during a career, a few stand out in grand fashion from the others.

My first meeting with Abe Lastfogel was one of those. I took the elevator to the top floor of the Beverly Wilshire Hotel and was let out to the entrance of a Penthouse apartment with a spectacular view, crystal chandeliers and Loretta Young sitting on the cream-colored sofa. I stopped in the doorway and took it all in – the city, the movie mogul and the starlet, their combined brilliance and lure blinding. It was almost theatrical. This never seemed to happen like this in New York.

Loretta Young and I exchanged pleasantries as Lastfogel invited me to sit and insisted I take a glass of Scotch. The starlet excused herself and I let my eyes wander as she said goodbye to the mega-agent. Statuettes and framed photographs of the day's power players lined the tables, trade magazines shouted bold headlines, undoubtedly echoing the fingerprints that Lastfogel had left all over town. The furniture was modern and clean, expensive, and I immediately thought about my own brush with furniture design.

"I think there's a place for you at William Morris," Lastfogel began immediately as he closed the door behind him. I studied him. He looked more tan than the men I dealt with back home and he was wearing loafers without socks, but I didn't let that distract me from the fact that I was face-to-face with one of the most powerful men in Hollywood. I nursed my drink and he took another. He explained that Benny had told him all about me. He wasted no time and offered me the helm of William Morris' London offices. The deal was laden with every perk you could imagine, every incentive you'd expect of a jet-setting life. I heard the details, but they got lost in my muddled thoughts of Sylvia coping with a move to Europe. I decided not to say anything to her about London right away, and somehow, I was dealt an out before I was forced to.

I arrived at the New York Morris office to meet the East coast head, Nat Lefkowitz. I told him all about myself, where I had been and how I ended up at this point. Nat immediately decided that I was far more valuable staying in New York where I was already familiar with the business and the local players. He made me head of the motion picture talent department.

William Morris gave me the perfect venue to use my sales skills, my overactive imagination, and my penchant for storytelling. I'd be responsible in managing and packaging some of the biggest names in entertainment. Rather than carrying around their pictures in a big book of studio stills, I now had them staring and talking back to me from across my desk. My role was to consult and strategize with actors, writers, and filmmakers, to make their names even bigger than they already were.

I started hitting the nightclub scene and brought Sylvia along with me to meet and scope out new talent. William Morris had me scouring the Manhattan hot spots and the boutique venues yet undiscovered in Greenwich Village. Sylvia and I were now regulars at these places, and she'd be greeted like royalty at the door as I scanned the crowd for the face or the entourage of the performer I had been sent to see. There were times when we were out every night of the week, ringside at the hottest shows in town. The agency's top brass would come out for the headliners, and we'd be dressed to the nines, wining and dining on the company dime, trying to remember the names of the City's socialites who invited themselves to sit at our tables. These were the days when there were cigarette girls and photographers on the floor, when drinking "booze" and getting decked out to hear a few songs were all very usual. A lot of these clubs were undoubtedly mob-run, siphoning money through its very long tentacles, but my job wasn't to know how the talent was being paid, it was to steal them away to come make more money with me.

The nights and years lingered into what seemed like one long club act. Even though Sammy and Frank were crooning within arm's length as Bobby Darin and Eartha did the night before across town, the names and the faces, like the energy and the lure, eventually became routine. It was a steady repertoire of days filled with studio heads, and nights with top talent in smoky clubs. And even if Sylvia wanted to stay home, I was still obligated to have my face seen in a club or two every night.

The culture of late evenings out didn't bother Sylvia as much as the one-on-one relationships I had to develop as an agent. I built my career unearthing diamonds-in-the-rough from the proverbial mines that had come to symbolize much of my journey. I was essentially employed to bring both unknown literary properties and the undiscovered perfect faces to screen. As the years and the faces got prettier, Sylvia began to express her displeasure with the demands and the nature of my work.

A young Swedish actress, who at the time was very popular in Europe, was in New York with her mother. I immediately arranged a meeting with both of them but not before I had one of the posh boutiques on Fifth Avenue send two designer handbags to their hotel room.

"What for?" Sylvia asked me over dinner that night. I had never in my life uttered the words Chanel and Hermès.

"I just want to pick the right one," I said. She studied me. "And you know best," I finished confidently.

Sylvia said nothing. I knew she trusted me implicitly, but my preoccupation with signing the young Swede was hard to ignore.

"Is she beautiful?" Sylvia asked. I chewed slowly, deliberately and nodded while I shrugged my shoulders to possibly offset the obvious.

At the same time I was courting the ingénue, another L.A. talent firm known for handling most of the sought-after European properties went after the girl. The platinum-haired beauty reached into her new handbag and pulled out the telegram. I read her invitation to come to Los Angeles.

Though predominantly situated on two separate coasts, it is an exceptionally small industry. The other agent knew very well that she was in talks with me, but rarely did that ever stop a talent agent from making his move. So I responded to the telegram. I sent a scathing, two-sentence wire that would surely clear up any possible misconception he had. I was mildly embarrassed seeing that kind of language in print, by my hand, but sometimes, these things have to be done.

Not long after the girl signed with William Morris, I received an invitation from Sweden to join the actress in Stockholm for a royal wedding. I would use the trip to meet her father and to discuss the agency's intentions with regard to her career. Sylvia and I attended the lavish celebration and had never before seen anything like it. Though the jewels and the gowns sparkled like a page from *Cinderella*, it was one image in particular that stuck with Sylvia.

Our hostess was young and fair and utterly stunning. Sylvia stood before her for the first time, the actress in a gold and cream gown, and it was impossible to pass off her looks as average as I had unconvincingly tried to do at home. The actress shook my wife's hand with long, gloved fingers and Sylvia stared at the creamy complexion that could only be described as flawless. Sylvia would later ask how any movie could possibly make her more beautiful than she was standing right there in person. I chose not to answer. The starlet kissed me on both cheeks, and though I had never in my life given Sylvia reason to doubt me, everything human in her at that moment undoubtedly would.

William Morris was *the* agency to sign with in town and the egos and reputations of the agents with whom I worked wouldn't let you forget it. Show business was strangely fascinating because it provided a place for everyone. No matter where you had been, where you were or weren't, educated, who your Uncle was or wasn't, if you were willing to play the game and could outlast the ones who weren't, you were in. Once they were invited into the building, Ivy League MBAs were on equal-footing with anonymous go-getters schlepping scripts and coffee in the mailroom. The agency was the Land of Oz, coming to personify the rest of the business as well. There was the lure of success — of meeting, discovering, representing or even *becoming* the man behind the curtain — the Wizard himself. In the end, after spinning your wheels, enjoying the perks and benefits afforded by the William Morris reputation and expense account, you realized that, at some point, you'd either get to the end of the yellow brick road or you'd wake up and find that it never existed to begin with. I saw so many young men get swept up in the what-ifs, often losing sight of who they were and why they worked sixteen-hour days. Men were pawns who had to navigate the office's political and hierarchal land mines, making strategic moves to coax their talent into making the most money in town. At the core of show business, no matter how magical the movies, is money.

I have always believed in starting work early in the morning. I'd get up with the sun and be in the office before anyone else. It probably came from sales days, when I had hours of driving uncharted territory to make my first appointment. Like any other day, I came into the Morris office very early and was the first to turn on the lights. I heard a shuffling of papers, the unmistakable metallic slide of a file cabinet and then silence. In the corner of the office of one of my colleagues I found various file drawers open and sheets of paper scattered on the floor next to David Geffen, a young agent assigned to the music department. He was on his knees in the dark. He didn't say a word, just looked at me as if I knew what was on those papers. He slid the last drawer closed.

"If I ever find you going through anything like this again, I'll break your jaw," I told him.

He was little, mousy, wiry even. He still said nothing, just slithered away. Later, we heard that David had signed some of William Morris' top talent to his own label with, as rumor had it, some exceptional leverage in his negotiations. I wasn't surprised at all.

Then there were the then unknowns that I remember fondly, the ones I still root for on my own. One in particular I saw for the first time in a very small theater on the East Side in a Sunday production of *Dames At Sea*. The curtain drew and the voice of an unknown Bernadette Peters cut through the room that smelled of a distinct mix of mildew and cheap perfume. With the rest of the audience, I sat up. No one had yet heard of her, but I knew it wouldn't take long.

After the performance I knocked on

Bernadette's dressing room door and found her even more petite buried under layers of costume and stage makeup. A trickling of guests made their way out as I introduced myself. I told her how impressed I was by her work and offered her representation on the spot. She was gracious and polite, telling me that she was entertaining a few offers and that she was happy to consider mine as well. I wanted to be the one to go back to the office and tell them what I had discovered, but part of me knew that I had overstepped the invisible boundaries that agents lived between.

I met with my colleagues in the theatrical department Monday morning and raved about the powerhouse I had spotted on the East Side. They indulged me, listening to my opinions, but quickly concluded the meeting by reminding me that decisions on theatrical talent remained exclusively with them. Had it been a simple issue of territory, I could have handled it. I knew already that it wasn't up to me to make my own offers to theater actresses on a whim. No, it was more than a boundary dispute; it was the everyday cruelty I saw that was catching up to me. They annihilated Miss Peters, dismissing her physical appearance, saying she was eerily small, almost disfigured. She was no showgirl, but to me she was better – she was the whole show. At that moment I regretted that I had ever mixed Bernadette Peters up with the agency at all. She went on to carve out a place for herself as a legend of the stage, and with each success and award the industry bestowed upon her, I secretly congratulated her on the much-deserved triumph in an altogether merciless business.

The life of an agent is very fast-paced, and I admit to sometimes letting the smallest issues cloud the big picture and Blessings of life. Yet, certain meetings always managed to put things back into perspective for me. I was sent out by Morris to go to the home of Rosalind Russell, who had garnered a solid reputation as a wonderful actress, playing in *My Sister Eileen*, *Auntie Mamie*, *Gypsy* and *Picnic*. I found her sitting on her old-fashioned porch of what looked like a two-story dollhouse. I introduced myself and she received me graciously and listened to my banter about representing her and making another picture happen for her. She didn't say much through the whole thing, just crossed her arms in the large sweater that was taking over her once delicate frame.

"I'm not doing any more pictures," she said quietly, but with a coolness in her eyes that meant she was serious. "I'm not well."

I didn't know what to say; I was paralyzed by her glassy stare. She smiled to let me know that it was okay, but I never forgot that meeting on the porch. I used it many times as a litmus test when I let my professional ambition cloud who I was as a person. Rosalind Russell was at the top of her game, one in which you fought fiercely to master. If she was vulnerable to letting it all go, what did that say for me? Here she was retreating to die from cancer and the very people she lived to please had little idea. Rosalind Russell showed me that it was as difficult to die a movie star as it was living as one.

You never think about your own mortality as much as when you are unsatisfied in any aspect of your life. The clock ticks louder, perhaps a little faster on some days when you know you aren't where you should be.

The first time I was exposed to death was as an eight year old boy in Philadelphia. An uncle died and the family positioned him on a dining table; I was absolutely terrified to be in the same room as his body. They ritualistically prepared him for burial and then there was a procession in the street from the house to the Synagogue. I was told to be proud for him, that this was an honor, but all I could do was try to get the sight of his white lips out of my head. *Would I have this kind of procession*, I'd think lying awake at night as a kid. *Would I be someone who warranted a parade?* Your thoughts don't change all that much from eight to eighty years old – instead of wondering if you'll get a parade, you wonder if your legacy will be that of reality or make believe.

Despite the new professional strides and the reputation I had developed that most young agents would kill for, underneath my exterior as one of the newest players in town, I was still the little boy from the Spruce Street Theater who was always replaying the dialogue in my head. Beneath the tailored suits and personal secretaries was a filmmaker who had never stopped loving the art of the story.

The structured life of the business of movies could only appease me for so long. I went from relishing the coup each time I secured a deal to secretly envying the talent that had put themselves out there. They were doing what they loved to do, and I was living off of their realized dreams.

I returned from London where William Morris was in negotiations with famed Broadway producer and director Hal Prince to secure the movie rights for *Cabaret*. We then negotiated bringing together Tony and Pulitzer Prize-winning playwright Edward Albee and Paramount Pictures for a multi-picture deal. The studio thought it was a good idea to bring the *Who's Afraid of Virginia Woolf* scribe aboard and William Morris would negotiate. After spending months securing the deal, I sat back and watched egos and the politics unravel what I had arranged. At this point, I didn't much care. I was on autopilot, closing deals and making stars, orchestrating careers I'd envied, all the while, dreaming up ways to be a kid again and surround myself with movies that people would never forget. As a salesman and agent, I was only as satisfied as long as the ink was wet on the deal. Once I cemented a place for the talent I was representing, I'd be on to the next negotiation.

Brokering and making movies are two different things. I'd had my share of dinners with directors who spoke more fondly of certain scenes they had conceived than the births of their own children. It's an indescribable feeling of satisfaction for a filmmaker to sit in the dark of the editing room and watch your own imagination unfold, just as it is for a writer to hear strangers quote the very dialogue they struggled writing during those solitary, lonely hours of genius.

I, too, wanted to taste satisfaction as permanent as the kind burned on celluloid forever.

CHAPTER 13

"It was the easiest deal I'd ever made. Howard Minsky believed in this supposed piece of dreck with such conviction that he resigned his position at the Morris office to go for it and get Love Story onto the screen. Poor guy.

By the time it got to me, he was a beaten man. I think, in all of filmland, mine were the last eyes to see it. His dance card still totally on empty, Minsky was quick to his knees to close the deal. I give the guy credit, giving up a cushy job to wildcat. Howard did and hit a gusher. A gusher so big that he never had to work again for the rest of his life."

> — Robert Evans, President of Production, Paramount Pictures in his biography, *The Kid Stay In The Picture*

At William Morris I worked with a lot of brilliant talent. I also waded through bottomless piles of scripts that weren't worth the paper on which they were printed. A script, in its own way, is like a new starlet that's just come off the proverbial Hollywood bus. Everyone knows where in town it's been, who's rejected it and who's made it empty promises of blazing success. It wasn't uncommon for a property of either sort to be passed around.

A script crossed my desk at the agency with its front cover mercilessly scribbled upon, like a sort of passport, documenting its difficult journey and reputation around town. I decided to read it that night, and by morning, I knew I was going to make this movie. I'm sure it sounds reckless and crazy for a man who was now in his fifties, whose subsidies from William Morris were astronomical and allowed us to live a very good life in Manhattan. If I abandoned the agency I'd lose my rent subsidy, paid parking privileges in the City, my incredible expense account, and most importantly, our medical insurance that was the parachute I hoped Sylvia would never again need.

It's a long shot that the right chemistry and luck will exist for a producer to shepherd a project through the various hurdles, mazes and hoops of production. Another, albeit big, strike against me was that I had never made a movie in my life. I read the script in April of 1969 and the next day I set a meeting with writer Erich Segal for five-thirty in the afternoon at the Red Coach Inn off the Boston Turnpike. I used the ride there to rehearse what I would say. I knew by heart how to close a deal for just about everybody else in town, but this one would require that I looked the part myself. I also began rehearsing just what I would say to Sylvia, telling her that I had quit my cushy job and was going to make a movie.

Erich was a relative unknown who was having trouble getting read. He had had two previous films produced, both with terrible returns. In agent-speak, that meant that he was a liability, but I knew that if I wanted to own this property I would have to convince Erich that I didn't care about his record, only about the story he had written. Good scripts go undiscovered all the time, either lost amongst the others or its potential suffocated by the writer's own reputation. I had no idea at the time that this manuscript, with rejection reminders scribbled across its face, would earn a place in movie history.

I found Erich Segal waiting with a clean copy of *Love Story* on a corner table at the Red Coach Inn. I'd heard around town that the young writer was frustrated with the rejections he'd been receiving, something he wasn't used to in his highly academic world as a Yale professor. Hollywood doesn't give a damn about what books you've read as long as you can make one that will sell. I made a few calls and it seemed the consensus was that the script read too corny and wasn't anything like the edgier, more provocative movies being produced at the time. I really didn't care. I was blinded purely by story, and like the twenty-three year old salesman in Kentucky, I pitched Erich his own story, the one that I envisioned on screen.

"I will produce this movie if you agree to make a few changes," I told him. I began bouncing ideas off of him. He noticed the tattooed cover of my script and I slid my hand over the graffiti while I kept talking.

"The father is a New York cab driver. I want that changed. Make him a baker, from New England."

Erich took notes.

"The mother has a foul mouth and is

altogether useless. Let's get rid of her. It makes the relationship between the daughter and her father stronger without her. Take out the mother."

Erich listened.

"The family is Jewish. Make them Catholic. The conflict between the Yankee and the Italian works theatrically."

There was one thing worse than having a producer tell you to change your story – not having it produced at all. Erich was listening.

"And calm down the language a bit; that which is essential to story and character can stay. We don't need any for shock value." I locked eyes with Erich and shrugged. "That's it."

"That's it?"

"If you make these changes, I will produce your movie." Confident on the outside, the words rattled with uncertainty in my head. Produce a movie? What did I know about producing a movie? But one thing was certain: motion pictures in all forms had been my life. *Love Story* and I found our way to the Red Coach Inn for a reason and I knew it. Now all I needed to know was how I was going to tell Sylvia that I was making a movie, moving us to Boston, and leaving my job and all the security that came with it.

My deal with Erich was simple. The project was turned down by various agents at William Morris, so I had the clearance to purchase the rights, and all forms of the plot, from Erich for $100,000 and a portion of the producer's profits. I had no idea at the time that they would end up being astronomical. We agreed to be partners.

Sylvia knew exactly what this project meant to me. She had never before stifled my growth or the chances I took, no matter how they inconvenienced her. Yet, still the voice of reason, she reminded me that I had worked decades for the executive position and salary I had at William Morris and that whatever happened as a result of producing this movie, chances are I wouldn't be able to return to where I now was. The movie would change me one way or another and office life would never satisfy me again. I knew all of this; it hadn't satisfied me for a long time now.

Sylvia backed me without blinking. The paychecks would soon stop and we would resort to using our own savings right to the day the picture started recouping, if it did at all. My doctor told me that he'd diagnose me as crazy if he didn't know me better, that such a lifestyle change would either give me another sixty years of life or would kill me somewhere during production.

I was called to L.A. to have dinner with Abe Lastfogel and his wife Francis. We met at his country club and I felt a bit uneasy because I knew this meeting was meant to discuss my departure from the agency. Like he had done when he hired me in the fabulous apartment with Loretta Young, he cut to the chase, and before I ordered a drink, he began.

"You are making a very big mistake leaving Morris, Howard. I have big plans for you."

Francis was a former entertainer herself and she was as animated as he wasn't. She grabbed my shoulder and tugged it, trying not to roll her beautiful eyes. Francis was a tough bird.

"Do what's best for you, Howard, not what Abe thinks. Abe thinks for too many people," she finished sipping her cocktail. Abe didn't look like he agreed with her, but she continued nonetheless. "He doesn't want to lose you, but if you don't follow your instincts then you change the course of what your future could have been."

I never forgot her for that. It was very hard saying goodbye to colleagues and mentors who had carved themselves into the film archives, but I knew, as Francis echoed, that the future was what I'd make of it.

When I got back to New York, I saw Nat Lefkowitz and told him that I had dinner with Abe Lastfogel. Of course, as the head of the office, word had already reached Nat long before I landed back in New York. I told Nat that I'd like William Morris to represent *Love Story* and he shook his head and said that when somebody leaves William Morris, they leave for good. Nat Lefkowitz was not a bitter man, in fact, he was good and kind and I knew that hearing about my departure was a blow to him. I didn't blame him. A few days passed and he called me into his office. He told me that he would helm representation of *Love Story* and would work to place it at Paramount Pictures.

I will admit that I have gone through life with others accusing me of being too happy-go-lucky and just too damn nice. I remember when we were shooting the picture, having people ask each other if my Boy Scout act was for real. I even heard that it made some people uncomfortable. It was David Golden, from whom I absorbed the art of producing, and Arthur Hiller, our director, who stuck by me. David Golden was a good man and a very good producer. And though I wasn't conscious of any Boy Scout act, I never really saw the point in trying to live any other way to please the cynics and critics that come for free in my business. I grew up during the Depression, lived amongst the coal miners, moved my family to a dozen cities and lost many years with my wife to severe and debilitating depression. There was no point in making life any harder or any more serious than it already was. I was neck-high in miserable people trying to step on each other for a glimpse of the top, and there was no way that I was going to leave that as my legacy in this business. So if I was now the Boy Scout on the set, so be it.

Paramount Pictures had an option on Ali MacGraw who had just come out of a successful movie called *Goodbye Columbus* and who had caught the eye of Bob Evans, head of Paramount production. I learned through Marty Davis, a friend and assistant at the studio, and future Paramount president, that Ali was available to do a movie. I contacted her agent and set up a luncheon at The Ground Floor restaurant on Sixth Avenue.

The first time you met Ali MacGraw you knew exactly why she was a star. She glowed. She just glowed. She was articulate and charming and over the course of our meeting I saw both the sharp edge and the soft girlishness that I would need in my lead role. I explained the part to her, explained the rewrites and the direction I envisioned. She read the script before our meeting and told me that she wouldn't do another film until she played the part of Jennifer Cavalleri. We made a deal on a handshake and she kissed me on the cheek. Our next meeting was coffee at the Plaza. I brought

Sylvia and Ali brought with her a very handsome young model with whom she was living. She was wild about him and told Sylvia all about it over the meeting. She was young and had already been married once; she had quite a bit of flower child left in her. I could tell that afternoon that they were a gorgeous couple, but that there would be no place for him in the wake of her inevitable stardom.

I arranged for Ali to leave New York for Los Angeles to meet Bob Evans and the powers that be at Paramount. We flew to California and Bob had a limousine waiting for Ali that would take her to The Beverly Hills Hotel where a private bungalow was set up for her. She only brought a single bag, in fact, I think she only had one dress. It didn't matter because Bob arranged for her to be escorted to L.A.'s best shops where she'd be able to buy anything she wanted. This was the beginning of Ali's whirlwind courtship with Bob Evans, but it was also all the leverage I could want in garnering interest at Paramount; she would soon marry the head of production and he would end up green-lighting *Love Story* because his new bride *just had to* be in the movie.

This wasn't the first time that my path crossed that of Bob's. As an agent in Hollywood many heavy-hitters call you for your clients' information, but no one ever went as far as Bob. He was a very good-looking man, powerful in the business and wealthy not just from pictures, but from his family. If he wanted a date, he usually didn't have trouble securing one. I got a call from him while I was at William Morris. He had seen a client of mine in a movie and wanted me to get the girl to go out with him.

"Look, Bob, I'm not a pimp," I said. His reputation was legendary. "Don't ever call me for this." He must have brushed it off, even confused me with the countless other flesh peddlers in town he probably called, because he never brought it up when our paths crossed again. Everyone knew that the agency-as-dating-service was one of Bob's most notorious M.O.s.

I now had Ali but would have more trouble securing the director. My first choice was Arthur Hiller, but when I sent him the project, he called back to tell me that it was way too corny for his taste, that the characters were one-dimensional and that he didn't think it had a place in the market. He was leaving on vacation with his wife to China and I insisted that he just take the script with him, have her read it and not give me a final decision until he got back. The salesman in me had resurfaced. Arthur called me when he got back and told me that his wife cried all four times she read the material. I didn't say anything then, but I knew from my early theater days that women audiences were a box office cornerstone. Crying was very good. With consult from his agent Phil Gersh, Arthur agreed to direct *Love Story*. He was in between two other Paramount films, *Plaza Suite* and *The Out-of-Towners*. He'd do my movie in between, and though it paid him virtually nothing in the beginning, signing on at a quarter of his customary fee, he made out okay in the end. Once production started, Paramount asked Arthur if he'd drop his salary another $25,000. As it was, everyone knew the studio was in financial trouble. In exchange for $25,000 of Arthur's up-front salary they gave him points, or essentially, a part of the profit. At the time the studio negotiated our agreements, they didn't think the picture stood a chance. When all was said and done, Arthur made a very, very good deal.

Initially it was Larry Peerce who was slated to direct the movie, or as he called it, the "piece of shit." I remember a story session we held in a hotel suite in New York. It was Peerce, Erich and myself. The two of them ripped into Erich's story and we ended the day accomplishing little except revealing that both Erich and Larry had strained relationships with their fathers. Larry didn't marry a Jewish girl and his father ostracized him; Erich was always at odds with his dad.

The similarities between Erich and Larry Peerce weren't enough to salvage the professional arrangement. Peerce went back to Paramount and made it clear that he wanted to bring in another writer. I vetoed that idea, honoring my partnership agreement with Erich, and that was the end of Larry Peerce. The job was then offered to Tony Harvey who was basking in the new success of his *The Lion in Winter*. It didn't work with Tony either.

David Golden, production manager for over thirty years, who would ultimately end up as Executive Producer on the film, budgeted *Love Story* at a very low figure for 1969 – two million dollars. Charles Bluhdorn, president of the studio, called me into his office and threw the numbers onto the big oak desk in front of me.

"Minsky, I understand you want us to finance *Love Story*," he said. "We want to do the picture, but you're budgeting way too high." I kept my hands clenched the whole time. I knew from the moment he threw the budget down the way he did that I was going to have to fight to get Paramount.

"And unless you can bring it in for 1.6 million, I don't think we'll do the picture," Bluhdorn threatened. I had never produced a movie, but I'd sold enough hot air to recognize it even in the fanciest of offices.

"Charlie," I thought I'd cut to the chase and call him Charlie right off the bat. "Charlie, if you want to play hardball with me, I'm willing to play hardball."

Bluhdorn raised his brows, thinking maybe I knew more than what was buzzing around town. Everyone was scared of Charlie Bluhdorn. He was an intimidating man and came with a hell of a reputation. He was an Austrian-born businessman who turned his garage supply business into the multi-million dollar Gulf + Western empire and bought Paramount Pictures.

I fingered the stack of papers in front of me and pushed them back so that they were now on his side of the desk.

"I don't want to make a television show. I want to make a movie. I own this property; it's mine. If you don't want to finance it for the budget that your own people made up, then I'll take the picture elsewhere."

I've been called lucky more times than I can remember, and I suppose the climate at Paramount and in America as a whole lent itself to making a movie like *Love Story*. Not only were audiences ready to escape from the tight noose of heated political debate during the height of the Vietnam

War, but financially, Paramount was neck-high in bad deals. They had over $100 million dollars invested in a slate of films and word was trickling in that their big budget, $23 million version of *Paint Your Wagon* starring Clint Eastwood and Lee Marvin was a desperate and humiliating flop. Rumor had it that parent company Gulf + Western was ready to pull the plug on Paramount in 1970.

Bluhdorn looked at the papers, then back at me. One word led to another and within a half hour an agreement was reached. Paramount had just taken on *Love Story* and Howard Minsky.

With the female lead cast, Paramount agreeing to distribute, and a director secured, I had to start thinking about finding the male star.

Through Paramount's casting office we tested just about everyone working at the time. We saw Michael Douglas, Jon Voight, Beau and Jeff Bridges, Michael York, Michael Sarazin, Peter Fonda and Keith Carradine. Not to mention, Arthur Hiller's favorite, Christopher Walken. I flew to San Diego where Walken was doing Shakespeare on stage and brought him to Los Angeles for the screen test. Arthur really wanted him for the role of Oliver, but we had to test all of the contenders in the same love scene with Ali MacGraw. They were instructed to kiss her, and though none of them seemed to mind, not all of them connected with her on camera. It became clear during the auditions that genuine sparks were exchanged between Ali and one particular young actor. After reviewing the tests, the undeniable chemistry was confirmed. As much as Arthur didn't want to work with Ryan O'Neal, the television actor who had made a name for himself on *Peyton Place*, he was offered the role of Oliver Barrett IV, Ali MacGraw's on-screen soul mate. For his work, O'Neal would get paid $25,000.

I wanted Ray Milland, Oscar-winner for *The Lost Weekend*, for the role of Oliver Barrett's Harvard-bred and emotionally disconnected father. Milland's agent arranged the meeting and I opened by telling Ray that he would be a changed man in more ways than one after *Love Story*.

"No toupee," I told him.

"Howard, I never work without a toupee."

"This is a new career for you." I was being serious. "You'll never wear another one on camera again."

He thought I was nuts, but Ray took the part, sans toupee, and never again wore one on screen after playing Oliver Barrett III.

Erich Segal suggested John Marley for the role of Ali MacGraw's on-screen father, Phil Cavalleri. Marley had been in the picture *Faces*, and I agreed with Erich that John had the right face for the role.

The elements began to fall into place. Left behind were the days corralling the neighborhood kids into a Minsky West Philadelphia neighborhood play; long ago were the days in the Oldsmobile creating intricate storylines and characters from the top of my head to sell a picture that wasn't yet conceived back in Hollywood. While balancing the business and the politics of making the film, I began to see traces of something special on set; I knew in my heart that this was becoming more than just a sweet love story. The studio dismissed *Love Story* early on as a program picture, or second-rate film. I vowed to eat, sleep and breathe my role of producer to prove otherwise.

Love Story went into production just before Thanksgiving of 1969. Our production offices were located on West 44th Street, between Eighth and Ninth and we shuffled our resources from this location, back and forth to Boston and Los Angeles. As if we didn't have enough to worry about, Ali reported to set with a very dark suntan. Six weeks before we started shooting she married Bob Evans in a quickie ceremony in front of a judge in Palm Springs. They were rumored to have been in Mexico for a late Honeymoon, but as everyone else was swept up in the new Mrs. Evans, Arthur and I convened and tested her on screen to see if her skin tone would work for a Cambridge co-ed who was far from the beaches in dreary Boston. We'd have to rely a lot on make up, though Ali didn't naturally require much at all. She preferred not to be made up, but we'd need to work on her glowing skin, especially in the scenes where she lay dying in a hospital bed. The only other changes in Ali that warranted any cause for concern was the fact that, all of a sudden, her normally flat chest ballooned. Her breasts became the focal point of on-set chatter and even her own good humor. We soon learned that she was pregnant, and wardrobe had to be specially fitted to hide Jenny Cavalleri's quickly changing curves.
The cast and crew set up in Boston with a backdrop of Harvard and Radcliff Universities. No one had ever used the Harvard campus before to shoot a movie. I thought that this was as good

a time as ever to bring perhaps the most famous college campus in the world into show business. I arranged a meeting with the President of Harvard to secure permission to shoot on campus. I asked him to read the script, and as I had expected, he came back with some reservations about the language. I could see that he was a well-spoken and fine man, and I made a concession that we would eliminate much of the superfluous swearing that held up his approval.

"Certain words and subject matter have to be in the story, despite how objectionable," I explained. And in a brief lesson on character development and storytelling, which I was sure this scholar already knew, I explained how choices of speech and language defined many of the characters. An agreement and understanding was reached and we had secured the first green light from Harvard to shoot in Cambridge.

Love Story was off and running, and slowly, as the days and months passed, everyone on the picture began to realize that this film, dismissed early on as B-rated, was something special. Talk ensued in Boston and leaked back to Hollywood that what was happening on set was a magical gelling of cast and crew, script and emotion. I had known it when it was only words on paper, but as I sat to review every daily, I watched the lives of two young, ill-fated lovers begin to take shape and claim their place in box-office history.

Arthur Hiller would refer to me as the "midwife of *Love Story*," and I suppose I felt like one. I know there were times when Sylvia would have liked to see more of me, even when I was right there in front of her, but I admit that I was consumed with every detail of production. On one end, I was in filmmaking boot camp, on the other, I was assuring studio heavyweights that we'd deliver on time and within budget. Some thought I was delusional and that brings to mind my first meeting with the unit publicist on the picture, Nicholas Meyer. Meyer has since gone on to become a successful writer and director, but when I met him he was getting his feet wet on his first assignment helming all the PR for the movie. He was sitting across from me and was scribbling notes as he assembled my bio. He asked me what exactly I thought would become of *Love Story* and why I had garnered a reputation all over town as refusing to give up on something that had been read its last rites by more than one studio. I told him to wait and see. He, too, must have thought I was crazy.

I was on set every day and knew that some of the crew members thought I was in the way. I'd review dailies with Arthur after an already grueling schedule keeping the studio happy and managing my responsibilities of securing rights, certain insurance policies and completion bonds. I was hands on, yes, but I knew no other way. I'd been accused of wearing blinders, unwilling to let anything sway my course, even if others saw the potential risk or humiliation. I couldn't afford to listen. My blinders would be both my Blessing and my curse. On set, I may have been in the way of the veteran moviemakers, but I wasn't moving aside for anyone. I had my entire life and bank account wrapped up in this project.

My relationship with Erich Segal had

become tarnished by this point. Our handshake at the Red Coach Inn and the deal I made him both financially and by not allowing Paramount to swap him for another writer had come to bite me and leave a scar. I was a strong believer in publicity and hype in business – I lived it on the road. I knew that if an audience was waiting for something, its arrival would be more than a release, it would be a phenomenon. I told Erich that he should adapt the *Love Story* screenplay into a book. If we could manage a *New York Times* review, our chances of creating said phenomenon would be secured. Erich agreed to adapt the story into a book, the reverse of what usually happens with bestsellers. Our deal had already been made back on the Boston Turnpike. When I agreed to pay Erich, I paid for his story and all the rights to that story. He would continue, in turn, to receive very handsome royalties – a deal that many writers still don't manage to leverage today. When it came time for Erich to sign the Production/Distribution agreement for Paramount, the document that would essentially grant our permissions to Paramount to move forward in releasing the picture, Erich refused to sign it. He said that until I released my stake in the book version of *Love Story*, he wouldn't sign the agreement. I had Paramount waiting to release the movie, millions at stake for everyone involved, and I was being choked by my own faith in a person who was blackmailing me. I was backed into a corner and had no choice but to release all control of the book rights to Erich. The book was published in February 1970, a few days before we finished principal photography of the film, and though it was reviewed by the *New York Times'* Vincent Canby as differing the movie only by the printed "he saids" and "she saids," it went on to be a runaway success – on the *Times'* bestseller list for over a year, forty weeks of that as number one. It sold millions upon millions of copies and I felt strong-armed and cheated out of my right to be involved with its successes.

Erich's manner changed drastically from that of the young man I met in the diner who couldn't get a serious read anywhere in town. On set, he had little to do with anyone, often making the others feel as though he couldn't even see them, as if his Ivy League pedigree censored useless Hollywood sorts. Nick Meyer sums it up best in his PR memoir *The Love Story Story*:

"I discovered something very interesting about Erich Segal: if he wasn't talking, he had nothing to say. Which is to say, he wasn't interested in what anyone else had to say. In fact, so far from being interested, he was absolutely unequipped to hear any speech that did not pertain to him directly, either as a question or else as some form of unbounded admiration. I have said earlier that I discovered no egomaniacal directors or stars working on Love Story. This is true. But there were egomaniacs involved with the film."

As the shoot progressed, others noticed the same. Some of the only interaction many of the crew had with Erich was when he announced to as many people as would listen that a female visitor was coming up to his room while we were in Boston. The next morning he made a concerted effort to have others meet him at his room where they'd find the bed sheets torn from the mattress and the pillows on the floor. It didn't look like the remnants of a lovemaking session – it looked like a terrible monster had devoured the bed. The talk of the set remained this elaborate attempt to ward off the rumors of possible homosexuality. I was sad for him, because it only got worse. It wasn't helped by the fact that his mother regularly came to set wearing a large, custom-made button that said "I'm Erich Segal's mother." It was fodder for the crew, so everyone did as she suggested and called her "Erich Segal's Mother."

Years later I was approached by the new hierarchy of Paramount Pictures in a meeting at the Plaza Hotel in New York City. I was asked to release my permission to do a sequel to *Love Story*. I read the script penned by Erich and I wasn't committed to being involved, telling them that I didn't think it would recoup its negative cost. I gave the studio my okay along with conditions that I would earn a percentage if the movie brought in certain numbers I projected in my mind. They went on to cast Candace Bergen with Ryan O'Neal in *Oliver's Story* and it would ultimately be a terrible flop. Word trickled back that after our meeting in New York the executives had reconvened in Los Angeles with Bob Evans and got a terrible kick out of the fact that Howard Minsky released his clearance so easily and without a fight. They obviously didn't know by then that I never fight for anything I don't believe in.

I'd heard that Erich made a deal with Paramount and required a huge advance for the sequel. Paramount acquiesced, but under the condition that if *Oliver's Story* didn't earn, he'd repay those advances through his *Love Story* royalties. And how Hollywood collected.

One of the funniest stories I heard in the wake of the *Love Story* release was when Erich Segal put out a statement denying the claims made by then Vice President Al Gore and his wife Tipper. A December 1997 *Time* magazine article about Gore prompted Erich's statement and a good deal of flack for the Vice President and his wife. *Time* reporters Eric Pooley and Karen Tumulty published the following observations in the magazine:

"Around midnight, after a three-city tour of Texas last month, the vice president came wandering back to the press compartment of Air Force Two. Sliding behind a table with the two reporters covering him that day, he picked slices of fruit from their plates and spent two hours swapping opinions about movies and telling stories about old chums like Erich Segal, who, Mr. Gore said, used Al and Tipper as models for the uptight preppy and free-spirited girlfriend in Love Story."

I, just about everyone in Washington, and anyone who knew the origins of this picture were entertained by this for quite some time. While on a sabbatical in 1968, Erich knew the Gores and the Vice President's then roommate and the actor that would eventually be cast as Oliver Barrett's roommate in *Love Story*, Tommy Lee Jones. Segal later said that Ryan O'Neal's character was partly modeled on both Gore and Jones. The only element that Erich attributed to Al Gore was that of having a controlling father who expected that his son follow in his footsteps. Erich would later say in a 1997 interview with *The Dallas Morning News* that it was Tommy Lee Jones "who inspired the side that was the 'tough, macho guy who's a poet at heart.'" And Tipper, according to Erich, didn't inspire the female lead at all.

I've been asked many times over the years if I knew from where Erich drew inspiration for the characters in the story. Undoubtedly, many elements came from his time at Harvard; he's even said that he knew a couple like the one played by Ali and Ryan while at school. However, I spent a lot of time with Erich in story sessions and meetings, fleshing out these characters. I've always believed that much of Oliver Barrett IV was really Erich addressing his deep, strained feelings about his own father.

I'd like to be able to call the whole production experience seamless, but in reality, it took quite a bit of luck on our side to make it happen. For instance, while shooting in Boston, there was a post office strike that halted all mail delivery to Cambridge. Eastman had shipped the film needed to finish the picture and there was no way to get it. If there was no film, the movie would be forced to shut down. With pressure from the studio to stay on time and on budget, we did the only thing that we could.

I had to get permission from the Post Office, and escorted by a representative, a crewmember and I sorted through a warehouse of Cambridge, Massachusetts mail stacked nearly to the rafters of the building. We waded through thousands of letters and packages, and eventually, found the Eastman canisters that would be used to shoot the final scenes and wrap the picture. We were lucky.

After we wrapped, Paramount requested that we go back to Cambridge to get some more shots for story filler. During our trip, a snowstorm, heralded as the worst in twenty years, hit Boston with no forewarning and shut down production. Spirits were low and the relentless snowfall reminded most of the crew that they were far from home in Los Angeles. It didn't seem like we were ever going to get the pickups the studio wanted. As the crew lingered and the cast bundled themselves in their trailers, I paced the sound stage, running over the scenes that would now set us behind. The entire city was consumed by a blanket of white.

"Do we have a football?" I asked Arthur.

He shrugged his shoulders, this time really believing that I had finally lost my mind.

"Get it," I said and left to have wardrobe prep the cast.

That afternoon we shot one of the film's most memorable scenes with Ali MacGraw and Ryan O'Neal entangled in a playful game of catch on the powdery University football field. Chasing one another and diving into the snow, the two actors ad-libbed a lovers' game that would remain a key scene in developing their playful and spontaneous relationship. It would also serve as one of the pickup scenes that would satisfy the studio's request to pad the picture with more interaction between the kids and a way to spoon-feed the audience more reasons why the unlikely pair fell in love.

I wish that snowstorms and mail strikes were the most of our challenges, but it was clashing personalities and ego trips that marred an otherwise perfect shoot. Behind the goldilocks and white, toothy grin of Ryan O'Neal's all-American boyishness was a very troubled, violent and toxic person. In all fairness, he hated my guts, too, and he didn't hesitate to tell everyone so. In fact, in a press interview, he told a reporter that Howard Misnky's role on set was to pick up the shit Ali's dog, Grounds, left behind. And these were the kind things Ryan said about me. He didn't hide the fact that he resented being told what to do by a man who was making a movie for the first time. I suspected that the resentment went far deeper. I tried to befriend him right off the bat, to compliment him on his obvious talents and to remind him that he was a central creative force in the success of this picture. He ignored me right from the time I met him at his screen test. Whatever came out of my mouth Ryan interpreted as belittling, as my trying to strong-arm him as a decision-maker, even a father-figure. You didn't need a psychology degree to gather that Ryan had issues that stemmed from deep within, and his outbursts and degradation of cast and crew lingered as his legacy on the project.

Arthur had a tendency of re-taking shots that other eyes saw as perfectly adequate, but Arthur wasn't just adequate. He was a perfectionist and knew exactly what he wanted from an actor, a scene and himself. If he thought he had to do another take, he did it. It was part of his industry-recognized talent and a quirky part of his charm. Most of us respected it like professionals. I doubt many involved on the project would ever forget the exception. Arthur wanted another re-take and Ryan prodded him, insulted him in front of everyone and teased him about his personal insecurities, saying that they undoubtedly caused him to need more shots than necessary. Overcompensation. I called a break in the shoot and asked Ryan to follow me into a make-shift dressing room.

"You're performance is superb, but why do you have to mitigate it by treating Arthur as a fool?" I asked him as I shut the door behind us. "You're making him look foolish; you're making him look silly." Ryan looked at me with vengeance.

"Get the hell out of here! Don't tell me what to do! Get out!" he screamed. Our voices carried onto the set and became the talk for weeks. He opened the door and I pushed it closed. Others began knocking to come in and he'd yell at them to "get the hell away." I made the mistake of asking him what was troubling him and he grew even angrier, venomous.

"If you don't get out of here I'm gonna throw you out and that's after I beat the shit out of you. And you'll be off this project," he threatened. I had heard rumors that he was always pumped with drugs and it wasn't until this confrontation that I let myself believe it. I stood there, my blood boiling. *I quit my job and bought the rights to this project with my savings, and Ryan O'Neal wants to fire me.*

"You're not going to lay a hand on me," I returned. "You're not going to do a damn thing and you're going to stop this garbage with

Arthur." I opened the door and exited. He behaved differently on set after that, but the tension between us was even more palpable.

His highs and lows were legendary. His outbursts and arrogance were a marked contradiction to a very attentive and disciplined acting on set. He was a dichotomy of all the things Hollywood could bring out in you – talent and the deity-complex that comes with its validation.

When the picture wrapped, Ryan O/Neal sent me a scathing letter to summarize his feelings about me. It was undoubtedly fueled by Bob Evans' decision to pay Ali MacGraw a $100,000 bonus for her work on the film. Ryan got nothing. Though this decision came from Paramount, knowing Ryan and his sincere resentment of my financial gain from the project, he had more reason to dislike me. In that letter, I saw a grown man put into writing the pain unique to a hurt or scarred child. Grown men don't talk like that, but bruised men certainly can. I became saddened to know that he would go on to have a family without resolving his issues, and as I had heard over the years, treated them as he did those around him in his professional life. Ryan had a plate glass window in front of him — you could clearly see into it, see this handsome man who looked like the kid next door, but try talking to him or breaking through. You'd be left talking to yourself.

Nicholas Meyer summed it up again in *The Love Story Story*:

"Of all the principal figures involved with the making of Love Story, Ryan O'Neal is perhaps the most

complicated. If the others can be reduced, to general oversimplifications, to brilliant, ambitious and egocentric writers, romantic self-made businessmen, or unpretentious intelligent college-graduate film stars, O'Neal, even in this ineffective way, cannot. Perhaps this is because the qualities in the others' personalities, however contrasting, at the last all combine to make their owners effective, functioning human beings. One may or may not admire certain aspects of Erich Segal's character, but it must be admitted that these less savory attributes do not get in his way, Howard Minsky's eager-beaver romanticism, some may find cornball, but without it the "merely" good businessman that he was wouldn't have dropped everything and gone out on a limb to produce Love Story. With O'Neal, the case is different. Instead of combining to help him function more effectively, it appears that his contrasting characteristics are actively attempting to pull him apart, though he has struggled manfully in recent years to overcome the dissident elements in his personality. The struggle goes on; whether O'Neal will emerge triumphant in the battle for his soul remains to be seen."

The picture had wrapped and there was one more star that we had to cast before the film could be called complete, and that was the music.

I had never forgotten the way a haunting score filled the echoing canyons of the open-air West Virginia theaters, the way a chorus of notes could evoke as much emotion as the words themselves. Music, finely choreographed with a film, was as much a star as the actors themselves.

Erich Segal had brought his friend Charles Aznavour to the set in Boston and introduced him to me as the man he wanted to score the picture.

Erich's idea was that he, himself, would write the lyrics. Aznavour, who had an uncanny physical resemblance to Segal, befriended him while playing the French Olympic runner in *The Games*, the script Segal adapted for 20th Century Fox, which also starred Ryan O'Neal. The film was a disaster and Erich has been known to blame English director Michael Winner for ruining it. Erich threw an outright tantrum when Bob Evans told him that we were considering other composers. Aznavour was an exceptional talent, but Paramount had other ideas. They initially wanted Burt Bacharach to score the picture and we described to Bacharach the kind of music we wanted, even comparing the feel to the work of Francis Lai, the brilliant French composer who was known for his haunting musical fingerprints on *A Man and a Woman* and *Live For Life*. Burt stopped the meeting, saying, "If you want Burt Bacharach to do the music, then you get Burt Bacharach. If you want Francis Lai, get Francis Lai."

So we tried. Initially, Francis turned it down. In addition to already being committed to a Claude Lelouch film, Francis said that working on *Love Story* would require flying on planes, and he hated airplanes. Summer vacation was approaching and he wanted to spend it with his family. We heard all of his objections, but even with no way of proving it, we knew that Francis Lai was meant to be a part of this movie. Bob Evans had a very close relationship with Alain Delon, the French cinema demi-god who knew Francis very well. An arrangement was made for Francis to see the film in Paris; we'd fly to him. He later said that immediately after the screening, he went home to his keyboard and wrote the theme that very night.

He completed it that summer on the French Riviera where his parents had a home, and when the end of summer came, I took Sylvia to the small town of Grasse on the Cote d'Azur. Known for its perfume industry and flower cultivation, Sylvia and I had placed in our minds images of the fabulous Mediterranean retreat that was home to one of the world's greatest musical minds.

We arrived in Grasse to find Francis Lai in his parents' home, but rather than a barrel-roofed villa atop the cliffs, we arrived at a modest two story, two bedroom house with no windows, just tulle curtains blowing in and out of the squares in the walls. But somehow, in that simple environment, with a lingering salty breeze from the Mediterranean somewhere far below, the music that Francis began to play on a tiny concertina was even more mesmerizing. As if the house was taking deep breaths in tune with the emotions of the melody, the drapes heaved inward and out. I watched as the thin Frenchman closed his eyes and played with a regal confidence that transcended his body and the room. A tear in Sylvia's eyes broke and mingled with the perspiration from the Riviera summer, but nothing about the moment was uncomfortable.

As Francis opened his eyes and locked them on me for his approval, I threw superstition to the wind and said with no pause in my broken high school French, "Francis, when we have the Academy nominations, you are going to win the Academy Award. *Tu vas gagner! L'Award Academie!*"

Sylvia kicked me in the ankle.

"Why did you say that? How could you say a thing like that?" she'd say the minute we got into the car.

"Because it's going to happen," I replied as I navigated the two-lane road down from Grasse onto the coastline below. "Because it's going to happen."

It did happen. Francis Lai did win the Oscar for the very score he played for us in the house with no windows. I had always believed, and was walking proof, that it didn't matter where the hunger came from. Whether hidden in a kid trimming lettuce or a composer hidden in a flower-growing town in France, if it existed, it would be found. Francis Lai, and *Love Story* itself, were proof that great things can't go unrecognized forever.

That year, the British Film industry picked *Love Story* as the best film of the year and featured it at The Command Performance for the Queen. We arrived in London to attend the prestigious screening on March 8, 1971. Plucked from a storybook, the whole evening was surreal. Sylvia and I were briefed by royal attendants who consulted with us on everything from etiquette when meeting the royal family to our wardrobe for the evening. It was as if the moment was scripted by Hollywood itself. Princess Margaret received us as anyone would imagine a princess would, and then the Queen Mother surprised us all by dangling a hand-made lace handkerchief in my face and coyly giggling.

"Oh, Mr. Minsky, notice I'm carrying my hanky!" the Queen Mother quipped.

With the royal family in attendance, *Love Story* played the Command Performance in Leicester Square. I watched the faces in the theater staring up at the screen, every scene quietly echoing back to me that we hadn't done all that bad. I looked around as the audience watched the words that I had memorized by now, and knew that through it all, I had been granted an extraordinary courage and determination from the most prolific producer of them all — God. I had never produced a movie in my life, and now, somewhere there in the dark, the Queen Mother had her hankie that she had brought, in some way, because of me.

Ali caused a scandal in the British papers. They wrote scathing reports that she was blatantly disrespecting the Queen by wearing a brown tie-dyed pantsuit, black shoes and black gloves to the Command Performance. She was a gorgeous girl no matter what she wore, but that night she looked like a hippie playing in her mother's closet. I had heard that Halston made a stunning black dress for her for that night but that her new voluptuous, post-baby curves kept falling out of it. Apparently, the faux pas had nothing to do with the designer. Halston would later tell Evans that his wife kept falling out of the dress because she was wearing it backwards.

CHAPTER 14

Word quickly spread in the industry that *Love Story* was not the piece of dreck that my old colleague Evans had branded it. It was an "A" picture. On December 16, 1970 the film opened at Lowes 72nd Street Theater and Lowes State on Broadway, and for the first time, I saw my name in lights. It was intoxicating. *Love Story* took on a life of its own.

I was absolutely drunk with control, drunk with power, and I've never hidden the fact that it caused me to get an inflated head. I was fielding calls from every big name in town, names that I had known for years, who had laughed me off when I was peddling my project all over Hollywood. It was a good feeling and gave me the clarity and confidence I needed at that moment because I was being courted by just about everyone in town for my part ownership in the film. Bob Evans and his brother Charles, the business tycoon behind the Evans-Picone clothing empire, offered to buy out my private stake in *Love Story* the very night of the premiere. They had thought it through, and in the back of the lobby they offered me $3 million dollars to sell off my interests in the movie. The same kind of offer came from the owners of the Loews Theaters. It was one hell of a feeling thanking them and telling them with utter reassurance that *Love Story* was not for sale.

To better explain why my stake in *Love Story* became a hot property, I have to summarize my overall deal with Paramount. I had a property for which I paid $100,000 of my savings. Paramount agreed to put up the $2 million investment and would take whatever the film initially made until they recouped their two million. Everything above two million I'd split fifty-fifty with the studio and would pay Erich Segal a third of every dollar I made.

Being a new creative player had other perks that couldn't be quantified. While set up at Paramount, I got a new neighbor in the creative suites we used as offices on the lot. Mario Puzo had just written a book called *The Godfather* and was moving into the office next to mine to adapt it into a screenplay. His initial cut for adapting the book was $50,000. Bob Evans immediately befriended him, set him up at the country club, wined and dined him as Bob would likely remind you that only he could do. And in Puzo's office, Bob stocked his shelves with enough liquor to set sail upon. This would be where Puzo would write one of the greatest films Paramount ever put out. There was only one slight setback.

I was going over paperwork one evening when a faint tap on my door belonged to Mario Puzo. We exchanged pleasantries and discussed his project and his timeline. He was a well-spoken man, and later I learned that he was brilliant. He was a true talent who was a character himself, a little gritty, slightly intimidating and entirely dependent on his privacy and booze.

"I've never written a screenplay before," he'd tell me. I stared at him. We all knew that he was a genius writer who had the guts to put words and stories on paper that most would deny ever knowing. However, novels aren't movies, just like being an agent isn't being a producer, and I understood exactly what position he was now in. We engaged in the first of many talks about screenwriting and film. I, by no means, am a screenwriter, but I had been around movies, dialogue and my own script long enough to explain the nuances of the medium.

"It's a skeleton. It's a clean backbone of what the director will use to spark a vision. Not wordy, few if any flagrant descriptive passages, and no internal dialogue. Write only what I'm supposed to see," I said and handed him the *Love Story* script. "I make it sound easy, don't I?" We shared a laugh.

Screenwriting, good screenwriting, is anything but easy. It's a complicated marriage of images and an economy of words. The art in screenwriting is showing the entire movie in words laden with meaning and punch. A good script makes a good movie. A great script is literature on its own.

I enjoyed having Mario Puzo as my neighbor at Paramount, and the linger of cigars and Scotch is something I'll always equate with his genius. He invited me to his home on Long Island and told me that he was going to fix me the best spaghetti I'd ever had. Sylvia got a kick out of the whole night, and I have to admit that his spaghetti was almost as good as his movie. Over an after-dinner glass of Sambuca with the requisite three coffee beans, I offered to produce Mario Puzo's next picture following *The Godfather*. He was interested to hear the details I had drummed up. I was offering him a far bigger stake in his own creation than any studio would give him at that point, but he told me that he had contractually bound himself to Paramount. I enjoyed the company of Mario Puzo, and when *The Godfather* came out, I secretly wondered just how much of that material he had created and how much he had seen with his very observant eyes.

One of the producers of *The Godfather* was a man by the name of Al Ruddy; he was a very good friend whom I admired and respected. After the release of *Love Story* and its underestimated box office performance, news trickled back that Bob was indeed making claims on the picture above and beyond his usual. He was notorious for confusing the role of head of production at the studio with the people on set who actually saw the picture through to completion. He'd smudge the actual fingerprints on the films Paramount made while he held his office; he wasn't shy about being the self-proclaimed reason behind *Love Story*, *The Godfather*, *Rosemary's Baby* and *Chinatown* to name a few. It didn't bother me like it did some exceptionally talented colleagues of mine who also nearly bankrupted themselves and ostracized their families while seeing their pictures through. People in Hollywood want to be associated with a winner. No matter who's responsible for a losing property, you won't find them lined up to take credit. No one stood in line to take credit for *Paint Your Wagon*. But if you're a hit, everyone's around to cut the cake.

Nick Meyer in *The Love Story Story:*

"Certainly Peter Bart, Paramount's West Coast intellectual-in-residence, was wrong when he stated in Time magazine, after the film had become a box-office bonanza, that Evans had developed a mania on the subject of the film, that he was on the set every day, and that he insisted on cutting the picture himself. Evan's own statement in the magazine's same number was closer to the truth: he saw in the film a nice little "trend-bucker," but a bonanza? "No way." Only Minsky seemed to have been granted this sublime vision into the future. As for Evans' constant presence on the set... it was not until principal photography was completed in February, by which time Segal's novel of Love Story was climbing steadily up the bestseller charts, that Evans appears to have become personally involved with Love Story, beyond an understandable interest in his wife's performance."

Al Ruddy asked me about Bob and about the news already trickling in that Evans himself was touting "his" property *The Godfather.* I could see the frustration brewing in Al; I knew what this project meant to him, to his partners and to my neighbor Mario who would spend late nights pounding away at the typewriter like a tortured soul. I smiled and just offered Al two names: an accountant and a good PR man.

"That's all you need to get through it, Al."

On my own front, it took me quite some time to sanely filter through the myriad of reports that everyone and their mothers were responsible for *Love Story*. I have always acknowledged that it was a team effort, a brilliant choreography of talent, timing and Grace that allowed us to release *Love Story* at a time when audiences needed an emotional release. I nearly bankrupted my family because I believed in this. Those looking in say I hit the financial gusher of a lifetime, and I agree that *Love Story* ended forever our days of filling envelopes with my modest paychecks. But to me the gusher I struck didn't rain money — it rained every memory I had stowed away since passing out flyers for the Spruce Street Theater, making it so that I could sit alone with the singing cowboys with whom I had truly, truly fallen in love.

CHAPTER 15

Paramount Pictures was always blessed by the presence and genius of Adolph Zukor. He was president, chairman and fundamentally the creator of the Paramount Pictures Corporation, and he commanded a respect within the motion picture business not only as a pioneer who started the penny arcades and nickelodeons, produced the first American-made feature film in 1914, and went on to foster the growth of a media empire, but as an immigrant who never lost sight of the very tangible opportunities hidden within the world of make-believe. He was the Chairman Emeritus of Paramount Pictures until his death at age 103, and even long after he had no official business on the studio lot, he had a wonderfully plush office and loomed the hallways to the pleasure of everyone who worked under the studio banner. He was a legend of an industry that he, in part, created.

As every one of my own years have passed, I think back to Adolph's 100th birthday party at the Beverly Hilton, a star-studded affair at which emcee Bob Hope quipped that if a bomb went off in the room, Hollywood would be wiped off the map. When Hope delivered the line, the room echoed thunderous laughter, the most recognizable faces in entertainment indulging one another at the thought of their indispensability.

I laughed with them, but my thoughts were preoccupied. I looked around, taking everyone in. I marveled being at that party, being a friend to a man who had reached the absolute heights of my very own dreams – touching everyone with his passion for movies. Somewhere along the way I had earned a seat aside Adolph Zukor as a friend and colleague. Mae West winked at the mogul as she toasted him, and we all raised our glasses with her. Paramount sold the candles atop Zukor's 100th birthday cake for $1,000 a piece and donated the money to charity. I was warm in the glow of the 100 candles, watching my friend make another wish, surrounded by the very pillars of the business he helped mold.

Adolph Zukor lived in New York where I used to go and spend evenings with him in his apartment. He'd show me things he'd collected on his trips around the world, photographs that echoed an army of friends, yet he seemed to be a very lonely man. Statuettes and plaques whispered stories of great distinction even though each passing year took some of those memories from him. Zukor was short and robust and he had an Eastern European accent as thick as the big Churchill that was always in his mouth. He was a straight shooter, and I admired how he didn't waste a word if he didn't need to use it. He was gifted at separating business from everything else.

George Raft was a very popular actor in such films as *Some Like It Hot*, *Ocean's Eleven* and *Around the World in Eighty Days* who also had a very bad habit of arriving on set hours late. One day Raft held up the staff and crew for nearly half a day prompting Zukor to come down to the set.

When George Raft finally meandered in Zukor asked him into his office and with his thick accent said, "George, if you were me and I came in as late as you've come in today, what would you do?"

George answered, "I'd fire you."

Adolph Zukor folded his stubby fingers, nodded his head and said, "That's right. You're fired."

George Raft was one of Paramount's biggest stars at the time, but Zukor didn't hesitate using him to make it very clear that no star shone too brightly to compromise the studio's best interest.

Adolph Zukor told me stories about growing up and knowing that he was meant for more than what society had branded him. He was born in Hungary in 1875 and immigrated to the United States, taking on the role of film salesman as his first job. I quietly enjoyed that parallel. These were the moments I preferred with Adolph Zukor, as many of the others were shrouded in business and protocol. While in Los Angeles I invited him to dinner. His accepting caused a whirlwind of curious speculation on the set and at the studio, with people asking one another why Adolph Zukor would accept an invitation from me.

He said one thing to me the night of his hundredth birthday that I've never forgotten.

"Howard, you made *Love Story*, but one day you're going to make something bigger and more important. Even you're going to be surprised." I've kept that with me, and every year as Blessings come my way, I think of him and know that life itself could very well be that great accomplishment. Everyday at noon he'd come into the company dining room and the first thing he had was a cup of grape juice. For as long as I knew him, the first thing was grape juice, undoubtedly followed by a cigar. He lived to be 102. I was very fond of him. Very fond.

That Christmas weekend, *Love Story* grossed more than any film had done before. People went to see it in droves with their tissues and handkerchiefs like snowflakes everywhere.

To secure an international return, Charlie Bluhdorn wanted me to promote the picture abroad. Sylvia and I got vaccinations we'd never heard of and set off around the world promoting *Love Story* in London, Paris, Rome, Berlin, Japan, Hong Kong, Australia, Taiwan, Saigon and countless venues in between. In Australia, where movies weren't played on Sundays in those years, an exception was made for *Love Story*.

Love Story, once dismissed by all the studios in town, was now being coined as "the picture that saved Paramount" from the financial troubles it was facing at the end of the 1960s. The film was nominated for seven Academy Awards. Francis Lai took home the Oscar as I had predicted in that tiny room on the French Riviera when Sylvia kicked me in the ankle, and the score was subsequently nominated for a Grammy. *Love Story* also went on to be nominated for seven Golden Globe Awards and took home five of them, including the honor of Best Motion Picture Drama. The American Film Institute has named *Love Story* number nine on its list of the "100 Greatest Love Stories of All Time" and selected the film's unforgettable line, "Love means never having to say you're sorry" as the number thirteen movie quote ever.

On the night of the Golden Globes, Paramount sent a plane to Palm Springs to bring me to the Los Angeles ceremony. Sylvia was too sick to be with me. Vincent Price opened the envelope and announced my name. It was as if, in that moment, I was suspended over the room; the thunderous applause and the musical score seemed to slur in slow motion and I didn't come down to earth until the plane landed back in Palm Springs that night.

All of a sudden it seemed everyone wanted to know who I was, from where I had hailed, and how I had become a movie producer. Though I loved the attention *Love Story* garnered, I was never entirely comfortable with the attention fame itself brought. It was one thing to deserve a pat on the back for a job well done, but I couldn't fathom why people wanted my autograph or a picture of a guy they've never seen before. They would call me at all hours of the night to ask me to explain parts of the movie in more detail. I recognized from my earliest days on the road that fans were the driving force behind any entertainment success, but in the years that have passed, have come to learn that people sometimes confuse fame for talent and accomplishment. I appeared on the Ed Sullivan show, and as if it wasn't embarrassing enough, exited the sound stage to find a mob of people waiting for autographs. I used to wonder if any of those people kept that slip of paper, and if they did, stared at it years later wondering who in the world

Howard Minsky was.

During the shoot of *Love Story*, as the film's early buzz crept back to the studios, I was approached to produce *Paper Moon*, a film that went on to win Tatum O'Neal an Academy Award at age ten. I read the script and turned it down. The language in the project didn't appeal to me; I thought it was gratuitous vulgarity for the sake of being provocative. Perhaps a bigger reason for my turning it down was that I didn't want to endure any more time with Ryan O'Neal, Tatum's co-star and real-life father. A lot of offers came my way, but behind my own curtains, an agonizing drama of my own was taking form.

Upon my return from promoting *Love Story* internationally, in 1973 I began production in Durango, Mexico on a picture called *Jory*, the story of a teenager whose entire family is murdered. Jory makes it his life's obsession to exact revenge on the killer with his own hands. Alone, and now responsible for his own decisions, Jory begins to mature and has to control his insatiable desire to find and kill the man who made him an orphan.

I saw Robby Benson on Broadway in *The Rothschilds*, and I was so taken by his talent and charisma that I asked him to take a meeting with me in Los Angeles. We began shooting shortly after and Robby was my star.

Spirits and morale were high on set, but on day two of shooting, a horse I was riding didn't want to go in the same direction I had intended. The horse took off and crashed into a tree with me still attached. My entire right shoulder was crushed, shattering my bones and any hopes of producing the picture. I was immediately taken to Los Angeles for treatment. *Jory* was going to mark Sylvia's debut as a film extra, but as soon as she heard about the accident she got out of costume and left her acting aspirations behind in Durango.

An ambulance waited at the airport and escorted us to St. Mary's Hospital in Santa Monica. Surgery was immediately performed, but I was advised to seek attention from a New York specialist. Sylvia would escort me back to New York where surgeons would rebuild my entire right shoulder.

Months later, the shoulder shattered again and the procedure had to be redone. While battling the excruciating therapies and rehabilitation and turning down offers to work again, I began to notice that Sylvia's condition was deteriorating. It wasn't anything I had ever seen in her, not even in her worst days lost to manic depression. They weren't the indicators I had come to know from the unregulated mania, rather these new symptoms were taking over her body in addition to her mind. She grew acutely lethargic, distracted, disinterested in the life that she had built with me.

My son Barry took over production in Mexico, and I was forced to live vicariously through his phone calls.

Something in me changed as I continued my therapy and watched Sylvia grow weaker. My lifelong obsession with the business of motion pictures began to escape me. Life would throw me a curveball, and though it broke my heart to admit it, I no longer had the energy to give back to make-believe.

In the middle of one night, I suffered a heart attack. Sylvia found me and I was rushed to JFK Hospital. A team of doctors descended on my bedside and Sylvia listened as they told me that quadruple bypass surgery was my only option.

The next few months seemed to blend into the previous few.

Hospitals, surgeries, painful recovery and back again.

CHAPTER 16

We set up home for the last time after our fiftieth anniversary. We moved for good to Palm Beach, and though we used to enjoy our winters in the slow and satisfying way down here, I began to notice that Sylvia was retreating from anything outside of our home. Her energy was gone. Friends in whom we had once confided wondered from the outside what had become of our lives. I lay beside Sylvia many nights and watched her stomach while she slept, making sure she was taking breath. She had done the same for me for decades, never once vetoing or sidetracking my dreams. So many times I watched her under her old white quilt and hoped that some of those dreams had been hers, too.

We found an angel in the caretaking of Martha Ramirez, a woman the likes of which, I often say, simply aren't made anymore. She watched over Sylvia night and day, and though I insisted that she focus only on my wife, Martha became my biggest caretaker and guardian in those very lonely times and to this day. It was Martha who would recognize the most subtle changes in Sylvia, the ones I sometimes chose to ignore, if only for hope sake.

Sylvia's hospital room was in a ward perched high in a building overlooking the

Intracoastal waterway that separates the exclusive island of Palm Beach with the center of bustling West Palm Beach. Pulling aside the bland, industrial drapes, I would watch the sunlight dance on the water and follow that dance across to the island where I had set up home with my bride. We started our married life here, with our paper-shell pecans and orange juice, and now, she was dying here.

After extensive testing and monitoring, Sylvia was released to continue her convalescence at home, but as the days passed, they took with them pieces of her. It wasn't long until we were back in the hospital for good. Like Sylvia had done countless times before, I packed her things, again placing her delicate clothes in the bag we had carried in and out of waiting rooms for as long as I could remember.

I spent many of the difficult days drifting the Atlantic Ocean on a twin-engine diesel that I had dreamed about for some time. I'd always have time to think on the boat, alone. Sylvia hated the idea of being suspended above deep, bottomless waters and hated the smell of the diesel even more. But now I was alone. I wanted this time to think about things as I drifted, but my imagination, once so sharp as to dream up stories with no boundaries, was now dulled by the years of replaying memories I was so scared to lose.

I passed time by playing captain to an elderly Palm Beach man and his nurse that I had invited for afternoons on the boat. I'd watch George Weltner stare into the water and smile blankly at me. I watched him lock his eyes on the churning of the waters and wondered just how far the Alzheimer's had deteriorated his fabulous memories. George's path had again crossed mine in Palm Beach decades after he took over as President of Paramount Pictures from my other former boss Barney Balaban. He would be the last president of the company before the takeover by Gulf + Western and long before I made my movie under their banner. It was George Weltner, a once laconic and sharp businessman, who toured my Philadelphia office on an inspection and would call me a week later with an offer to come to Paramount in New York City to become his assistant. I spent many mornings walking to the office with George, listening to his storytelling and savvy. I remember distinctly at one point during those conversations that George had let on that he liked boats; it's so vivid, it could have been yesterday. Strangely, here in the middle of the Atlantic Ocean, years later, the former studio boss who had taken a chance on me, was staring absently at the salty froth and didn't know at all who I was.

I stood, again at the window, explaining to Sylvia in the fatigued details left of my imagination how the trees were blowing in the wind, what the colors of the boats were as they navigated the waterway, how the clouds were casting pockets of shade over the parched, Florida cement. She'd ask me to tell her again about the water, about how I said it looked completely free and completely alive.

Marva Callender, Sylvia's incredible nurse and a woman whom I had come to depend on, peeked into the room, exchanged pleasantries with

Sylvia and asked me into the hallway.

The doctor was waiting. He closed Sylvia's door and motioned to some papers in his hand. He hesitated and I suppose at that moment he didn't have to say anything at all.

"It's not benign."

The words were lost in the squeaking and rolling of the nurse's cart that passed us. The words were utterly lost because I didn't want to hear them. I studied the man in front of me — white robe, dangling M.D. nametag, manicured nails and the stoic face he hid behind.

"What can I do?" I said.

The cart rolled by again, punctuating every throb of my head and broken heart.

I made no mention of the diagnosis to Sylvia. Perhaps that was wrong, but I wanted to be sure. Instead I told her that we were taking a vacation to the City. Barry would meet us there and Marcia would be coming in from Los Angeles, like old times. While in New York, I suggested we stop in and see some specialists I had heard about. First, we would see the kids, then we'd see some doctors.

At our first visit to New York Hospital, Sylvia was immediately admitted and Chief of Surgery, Dr. John Daley, scheduled a procedure to remove her tumors. As they arranged for the preoperative exams and preparations, Sylvia became aware, instinctively, that her trip to New York was less about getting away and more about confirming a last resort. In the days before her surgery, my wife and I talked about our sixty-five years together and we smiled as much as we could.

"I think you ought to do it now," the young doctor said, his eyes skirting the manila medical chart in his hand. I had been in the company of Doctor Daley's medical assistant a few times before, and I remember thinking that his boyishness was strangely pacifying. I'm sure it came in handy at times like this.

"It's a good idea that you not wait too long," he'd finish, leaving me to dissect the poised urgency conditioned in his voice. My mind had been severely dulled by a string of sleepless nights and the deterioration that comes with sitting up alone, trying to replay as much of your life in your head as possible and then trying to answer unanswerable questions against your better judgment.

The doctor's firm look coaxed me from my safe haze and I looked back toward the room that had become our home for the last couple of weeks. I was cemented to the linoleum floor – irretrievable seconds squandered in the terrible corridor lined with nothing but people like me, the loneliest kind of person in the world.

In the movies, the beeping of life support machines and the winding maze of tubes and gadgets seem like science fiction for someone who has danced in the sweeter arms of fate. These rooms and these things are a mysterious choreography of million dollar devices, but no matter what beauty you find in their purpose, ultimately, one wire keeps us going, and it seems, another shuts us off. More than once, I had watched prop masters tweak and manipulate the strangest materials to create the intense look and sound of a hospital room. My sound engineers would load me up with as many beeps and breathing tube gurgles that I wanted. Makeup would paint a veil of sickness and fatigue on the most beautiful of faces and at the click of the slate, old movie stars would effortlessly slip into sweet and simple death at the director's command. Producer or puppeteer, however I was seen, I had controlled scenes like this before. Only this time, as my own name marked the laminate door, there were no props or fabricated beeps, no actors or sweet, award-winning deaths. I was helpless and powerless and entirely at the mercy of God as I watched my greatest achievement slip away from me right before my eyes.

"Hi," her voice was heavy, coaxed by the littering of pills at her side. Sylvia was smiling and I knew that she was putting it all on for me. She'd keep it up until the minute I walked out the door, and I wondered what exactly she'd look like then. I touched her hand; it was attached to tubes that seemed to be attached to everything else.

"I've been thinking about you, Howie," she said, her face mirrored in my glassy stare. How I hated myself for letting her see her reflection in my eyes. "I know what's happening," she feebly squeezed my hand. "If I don't ask you now, I don't know if I will ever again be able to."

She swallowed hard and tried to smile, but in that moment I knew that this would be the most difficult question she'd ever ask me.

"Howie, would you marry again when I'm gone?" A tear broke and trickled down her face and disappeared into her cotton gown. I looked around. Sixty-five years of marriage and we ended up in this room. Sixty-five years seeing the world, raising a family, selling and making movies. She watched me as I studied every detail of the bed, the tubes, the medical bracelet on the wrist that I was used to seeing adorned with gold and diamonds. I touched her skin and another tear followed the first, becoming lost in the pale blue gown.

"Never," I said.

"I married a storyteller like no other." She feebly smiled.

I rested my head on her chest. It was bony and her breathing seemed like she was inhaling in doses, little by little by little. I swallowed the salty drops flowing onto my lips and wiped my eyes in one motion against her chest as I lifted my head from her body and looked her in the eyes.

"Never."

"I'm not coming out of this. I'm ready to meet Him. And when I do, I'm going to watch over you and hope that you don't forget me."

"We're ready for you," a calm voice interrupted from the doorway. I smiled to assure her that they were there for good reasons, but I felt like a liar.

I walked alongside her gurney until a subtle gesture from the nurses told me it was time to let go. Like it was just today, I still hear Sylvia's whisper linger over me.

"Howard, I will always love you."

And within seconds, I was left in that white, white hallway, cemented again to the linoleum, watching everything perfect and pure in my life turn the corner to nowhere.

CHAPTER 17

The quiet doctor extended her hand and her eyes brushed mine for a moment. Our handshake lasted longer than average, and I asked myself if she always did that with people like me.

The room was simple, more like a sparsely decorated den than an examination room, but I figured that was all intentional, to make me feel like I was far enough away. She pulled her glasses from her loosely gathered brown hair and shuffled through a file as I sat quiet, looking around and noticing no personal effects adorning the office. Why would they show you pictures of their families when this was the room where you came to give your own away?

"Doctor Daley has seen me and I've looked over Sylvia's files. I'm going to need to ask you some questions, Howard."

"To see if I'm crazy?"

"No," she said calmly, used to this.

She scoured the handwritten notes in the margins and I wondered what he had written there. Did he echo what he told me, did he write the words *galloping cancer*? Did he tell the young, quiet psychologist that he could have removed all of her insides as he told me?

"Howard, Howard?" She was looking at me, leaning slightly over the barren desk and I

wondered how long she had been calling my name.

"The Doctor explained to you that all of her bodily functions have shut down?" I nodded and she checked something off. How easy for her to check something off, I thought.

"And you understand that the team of surgeons has made the suggestion that her life support system be removed?"

Why the hell else would I be here?

In this room, cold in every way, I had an absolute stranger checking off the boxes of my entire life and happiness. She would need to determine if I was of sound mind and intention as I gave my blessing to remove my wife from life support. You read about these things; you don't live them. Not a day has gone by that I don't think about my signature sitting on that file. The doctor asked me again if I was sure and for some time I was so careful not to move at all, nodding even a trace, falsely assuring her that I understood or accepted what life would be like without Sylvia.

CHAPTER 18

>   JENNY
>   (to Oliver)
>   Close the goddamn door.

Oliver obediently goes to the door, shuts
it quietly. Moves towards Jenny's bed with
CAMERA now coming in TIGHT on them at her
bedside. Oliver looks at her, smiles.

>   JENNY
>   (softly)
>   It doesn't hurt, Ollie,
>   really. It's like falling
>   off a cliff in slow motion -
>   y'know?

Oliver nods "yes."

>   JENNY
>   Only after a while you wish
>   you'd hit the ground already.
>   Y'know?

He nods "yes" once more.

>   JENNY
>   (softly, smiling)
>   Bullshit. You never fell off
>   a cliff in your goddamn life.

He smiles. A silent pause. Oliver finally
hits upon a kind answer.

OLIVER
Yeah. When I met you.

— from the screenplay of *Love Story*, Paramount
Pictures, 1970

On November 11, 2002, Rabbi Shapiro's
words echoed off the stone walls of the Temple and
managed to comfort most of the hundred or so who
gathered there. For me, the poetic eulogy and all
of the Blessings reminding me to relinquish my
grief to God, for the first time in my life served
terribly hollow and inadequate in my head. For
certain, I could stay there all night and the next
day and until the last person would listen. I'd tell
them about Sylvia, about who she was and how
she loved me in spite of my long-time affair with
ambition, how she sobered me and tempered me
and how everything I called mine bore her every
fingerprint; but I knew that no matter how
beautiful a benediction anyone conjured at that
moment, nothing would change the fact that I was
no longer whole.

I leaned into the simple pine casket in the
center of the dark Temple and kissed Sylvia's
perfectly   red   lips   for   the   last   time.
Life imitating art seems so innocuous when
it's thrown around in conversation far, far away
from you. In the final scenes of *Love Story*, the two
young soul mates are separated by illness after

186

coming to terms with the vulnerability of their union. I'd watched the scene play out on paper and on set and in the late hours of the editing room. It made the Queen Mother and faceless audiences cry with the power of goodbye. Only now would the parallels and their depth come to truly haunt me. My mark in movies — some may say a single, lucky one, I say a Blessed and appreciated one, would forever represent an ambitious kid's foray into an uncharted magical world, forever represent a young and spirited defiance as onlookers discouraged and bet against me. My journey of incredible personal and professional highs would also come to symbolize everlasting love in a fleeting life. I believe in love, I believe in God and I believe in the goodness and purity of dreams. If I had never had moments alone in that dark and dated theater, taking in every word of someone else's dream come true, I wonder if I would have ever been able to spot my very own dreams. Some have called me a one hit wonder, others the luckiest guy they knew because I hit the proverbial gusher. However I am remembered, coming into my ninety-third year is a Blessing. If I am to be remembered only by my award-winning "one hit," it is, without question, my exceptional marriage to Sylvia.

The Benedictine and Brandy I mixed on the night I proposed to Sylvia when I was twenty-three years old was far more than an elixir of courage for me. It was far more than liquid sophistication for an innocent girl who had never imagined such a journey of ups and downs and back again. The Benedictine and Brandy of my life - bitter and sweet, biting yet warm, success of your wildest dreams and the lowest lows of loss and loneliness. I have tasted it all, and I will never forget the way one perfectly balanced the other. It will linger on my lips for a lifetime and longer.

NATALIE GARIBIAN PETERS graduated Magna Cum Laude from Duke University. She is an author and screenwriter and has been published nationally. She currently resides in South Florida.